What Successful Leaders Say about *Why Leaders Fail*

This book gives you what it took me 30 years of Navy experience to acquire. A must read for everyone, but especially those who want success as leaders.

—David Schiffman, Commander, USN (ret)

This is a must read for leaders and managers who are interested and motivated to excel, this book gives them a laser focus on the key issues Why Leaders Fail *and a recipe for preventing these issues from derailing their good intentions.*

—Irma Cota, CEO, North County Health Services

Why Leaders Fail *is not only a wonderfully prescriptive, valuable and essential leadership guide, it is truly inspirational. This book will not only aid the development of new leaders, but also reignite and energize experienced and successful leaders who may be losing their energy or leadership vision.*

—Dave Doss, CEO, Arizona State Credit Union

This book is the Sun Tzu's Art of War *for leadership. In the asymmetrical war of the business world,* Why Leaders Fail *is a weapon you must have to win.*

—Chris Heiser, Deputy Chief, San Diego City Fire and Rescue

Concise and comprehensive. Why Leaders Fail *is the go-to source showing not only leadership pitfalls but how to avoid them. This book is the keystone to being the leader you want to work for.*

—Skip Trahan, Captain, US Navy (ret)

This book is timely and timeless! Absolutely true and relevant! Thank you, Peter and Mary, for exposing the blind spots of today's leader and giving a practical blueprint to be great! It helped and inspired me as I am sure it will do for many others.

—David Horsager, author of *The Trust Edge*

Leadership is built on ideas like trust, caring, fairness, and vision, but business leaders often struggle with how (much less if) to implement these concepts in the real world. Kelly and Stark provide a compelling case for why these ideas matter and a fantastic guide for leaders to do the things that work in the real world to build loyal, motivated, and productive teams.

—David Dye, co-author of *Winning Well: A Manager's Guide to Getting Results Without Losing Your Soul*

The seven critical mistakes leaders make are explained in detail through colorful case studies and real-life examples. The valuable advice on how to avoid those issues and lead the right way is knowledge all leaders can benefit from.

—Randy Gage, author of New York Times bestsellers *Risky is the New Safe* and *Mad Genius*

Stark and Kelly give us an incredibly candid look at the blind spots that hinder our influence. If you want to avoid the quicksand that can derail your impact, find the courage to read this book and heed the advice of these two seasoned leadership experts.

—Kevin Freiberg, Co-author of *NUTS! Southwest's Crazy Recipe for Business and Personal Success*

It's great to succeed. It's what everyone wants to do. But often the really valuable lessons can only be found in failure. After all, as Yoda said, "The master has failed more times than the beginner has tried." Peter Stark and Mary Kelly have taken this counterintuitive knowledge to a new level and looked at how leaders have failed. From that uncommon knowledge, Stark and Kelly have assembled a fascinating treatise on how to succeed. Even if you think you've read all the books on success, do the smart thing and read the book.

—Bruce Turkel, CEO, Turkel Brands, Author of *All About Them*

Hindsight is still 20-20. Peter Stark and Mary Kelly have done every leader and manager a favor by looking backward and figuring out Why Leaders Fail. I first failed as a leader while still in my 20s and this book would have cut my recovery time in half! But you don't have to fail to benefit from their wisdom. Read this book, have your leaders read it and you will spot the warning signs before you get too close to the edge!

—Barry Banther, best selling author of *A Leader's Gift*

Although I have years of experience as a leader, Why Leaders Fail *was written for me!! It was a superb consolidation of key insights and nuggets of wisdom that are valuable to a leader or budding leader. I had several favorite chapters...including the overview about a vision and mission statement and the hands-on-steps needed to create each. Mary and Peter did an awesome job clearly defining how to develop both. Another favorite that is a requirement for anyone in a leadership position is the chapter on why trust is critical in the workplace and should be read on a daily basis!!*

— Linda Maloney, Captain, US Navy (ret), owner of Women Veteran Speakers and author of *Military Fly Moms*

Spot on examples of leadership failures that leaders at every level can learn from. A must read for future leaders or anyone who aspires to be "in charge".

—Steven W. Rakow, LtCol USMCR (Ret)

This book is a "nugget fest!" Typically, I read with a highlighter in hand, but it only took a few pages to ask myself, "What's the point?...every sentence is a nugget." It is so packed with great ideas, I found myself having little mind explosions throughout. I was also impressed with the writing. While there is excellent research, strategies, action items, and tips...it is also a very smooth and easy read. As an executive coach...this book has become my new "most recommended" to clients.

—Kevin R. McNulty, author of *The Gap Between Two Worlds*

Peter and Mary have employed years of experience to create a wonderful tutorial in becoming the best leader you can be.

—Donald B. Kearns, MD, President and CEO,
Rady Children's Hospital San Diego

If you're a bad leader, chances are your subordinates know it, but you don't. Stark and Kelly's Why Leaders Fail *will give you a refreshing jolt of reality and point out your flaws (if you're honest enough to see them). Alternatively, you can go work in a large bureaucracy for a decade or two and you'll eventually experience every type of leadership failure they discuss in the book. From personal experience, I can confirm that reading this book is a much less painful way to learn how to avoid bad practices that make leaders fail.*

—Len Cabrera, LtCol, USAF (ret)

Why Leaders Fail *inspires excellence! Outstanding read for all leaders at any stage of their careers. Excellent advice, relevant examples, and lists of ideas that will yield successful results.*

—Jane Moraski, Commander, US Navy (ret)

Excellent review for those currently in leadership roles, and a roadmap for those about to be.

—Chris Bahn, PhD

Why Leaders Fail *is more than theory or case studies. It provides clear action steps leaders can use to enhance their leadership skills and their team's success.*

—Pamela Jett, CSP, author of
Communicate to Keep 'Em: Enhancing Employee Engagement Through Remarkable Communication

Peter Stark and Mary Kelly provide a pragmatic guide that should be required reading for anyone in management, especially those who aspire to lead.

—Jon Peters, President, AthenaOnline.com

I've had the privilege of working with Peter Barron Stark Companies for more than 15 years and have eagerly awaited the weekly leadership updates as they hit my mail-box! In this exciting new book, Why Leaders Fail, *Peter and Mary share the key pitfalls that can derail a leader in today's extremely fast-paced and competitive world. The book also provides the tips we need to keep learning in order to increase our employee engagement—the cornerstone of all our success!*

—Ellen Schmeding, Director, Aging and Independence Services, County of San Diego Health & Human Services Agency

Why Leaders Fail *is straightforward and on point! I found myself identifying the great, the good, and the failing leaders I've encountered throughout my lifetime and the specific actions and habits that made them that way. This book is a must-read for any current or aspiring leader. Great advice for improving and building outstanding leaderships skills for any type of organization!*

—Paul L. Eller, Deputy Field Services Manager Colorado Division of Homeland Security and Emergency Management

Leadership is an art. Why Leaders Fail *will give you all the necessary tools to reimagine and create yourself into a great leader, if not a masterpiece of one.*

—Harry Paul, best selling author of *FISH! A Proven Way to Boost Morale and Improve Results* and *Who Kidnapped Excellence?*

This book is GOLD! This is page after page of fantastic leadership advice and wisdom backed up by case studies, interviews, and data. This is a GREAT book for leaders to read—not just once, but once a year, to remind them of all they can and should be doing to make their organizations, people, mission, and environment even better. If leaders (and prospective leaders) will read this book, it's going to improve a lot of lives—not just of the leaders, but of their followers and their bosses as well.

—Brigadier General Richard Fullerton, USAF (ret)

Regardless of your experience level, role, and workload, it is always good to take a step back and refresh your views on leadership... Why Leaders Fail *is a well written, easy read that allows just that!*

—Greg Ellison, Commander, USN (ret)

Not only do Mary C. Kelly and Peter B. Stark share powerful insights based on their years of experience working with C-suite leadership as well as managers in a variety of organizations, they communicate their big ideas through easily relatable analogies, examples, case-studies, and stories gleaned from first hand experience. This is a critical aspect of the book because so many leadership books will share the big ideas in a theoretical framework, yet fail to provide examples that connect to the readers' experiences. Consequently, people have difficulty relating the concepts presented to life as they know it. After presenting the "why," the authors then present viable and practical solutions that work to help the reader become successful as a leader.

—Susan G. Fitzell, MEd, CSP

Clear, concise, and informative. Relevant application across business and government settings.

—Hon. David R. Berman Kenosha County,
WI Circuit Court Commissioner

A very thought-out and in-depth look into what is lacking in leadership, and then they provide the easy steps to becoming a successful leader.

—Terence A. Rodrigues, E.Eng, GCertRSE, MIEAust

This book is essential for an emerging leader and valuable for an experienced one.

—Tim Durkin, author of *Moving from Promise to Performance*

Mary Kelly has been a leader in the military and as an entrepreneur. She tells it like it is in her speeches and her writing in an entertaining and informative way.

—Valerie Ormond, Captain, U.S. Navy (ret),
CEO, Veteran Writing Services

Why Leaders Fail *provides the reader with great examples of how to be a successful leader by avoiding the common pitfalls. The authors incorporated both leadership theory and practical examples in the book making it easier to apply the principals discussed. I found it to be a valuable tool in refining my leadership skills, and made it a must read for my entire leadership team.*

—Gregory Welch, Regional President, Northstar Bank

Not only is Mary one of the biggest hearted leadership experts I have ever met, but her ability to distill vital information and make it accessible is amazing. As business leaders and executives, our natural tendancy is to think we are already leaders because of our position. That is just not the case. Mary and Peter's book opens up new ideas on how to be better leaders over time and tactical practices to keep growing. Read this book as we always need to keep evolving as leaders in our own organization. This book is the key. I will keep coming back over and over to sharpen my skills.

—Heather Lutze, CEO, Findability University

Through Peter Stark's earlier book, The Competent Leader, *management in our credit union learned practical, deployable coaching skills to generate employee engagement, accountability and results. Now, in* Why Leaders Fail, *Peter Stark and Mary Kelly share practical and deployable methods to avoid critical pitfalls that can derail team communication, motivation and productivity. Adopting these simple, but significant, practices to make mindful changes will raise the credibility and success of all managers in our organization.*

— Geri LaChance, President and CEO,
SESLOC Federal Credit Union

WHY
LEADERS
FAIL

AND THE 7 PRESCRIPTIONS FOR SUCCESS

WHY LEADERS FAIL

AND THE 7 PRESCRIPTIONS FOR SUCCESS

Peter B. Stark | Mary C. Kelly
AS, CSP   PhD, CSP,
               Commander,
               U.S. Navy (ret)

Why Leaders Fail and the 7 Prescriptions for Success

Published by Bentley Press, Inc.

Peter Barron Stark Companies, Inc.
11417 W Bernardo Ct.
San Diego, CA 92127-1639
(858) 451-3601

Mary C. Kelly
4823 Ridgeside Drive
Dallas, TX 75244
719-357-7360

ISBN 978-1-935733-17-1

Book layout by e-book-design.com

Acknowledgments

Every speaking, coaching, writing, and publishing project we do involves a team. We are blessed to be surrounded by smart and motivated professionals. This project was possible because of the teams at the Peter Barron Stark Companies and Productive Leaders and their combined expertise, enthusiasm, and professional dedication.

Dusty, Marilyn, Donna, Kate, Julie, Jane, Marielle, Mika, Robyn, and Lori were patient and inspiring throughout this process, cheerfully reading and rereading multiple revisions and providing thoughtful edits and suggestions. We are fortunate they adopted this project as their own, and because of their vision and endless endurance, this book is a reality.

Our editorial and design team:

Chris Murray was a fabulous content editor whose ideas for flow and consistency helped us convey the right message in the right way.

Sandy Lardinois provided a wonderful grammatical review. The beautiful layout is credited to the talents of Gail Nelson.

Dedication

It is an honor to think about the selfless, wise, and truly great leaders I had the privilege of working with in the military. Lieutenant General Harold T. Fields exemplified the value of being direct. Marine General Hank Stackpole displayed how important it is for people to show up during times of crisis. Air Force Brigadier General Richard Fullerton possessed the rare combination of genius and compassion.

I have had far too many Navy influences to mention, but some must be included: Captain Gary Jensen; Captain Ed Waller, and his parents, Marty and Admiral Edward Waller, who once invited a 17-year-old girl to their house and changed my life; ADM Bob Conway; Captain Bill Rigby; YNCM Jiggs Franchi; and special thanks to my U.S. Naval Academy classmates for a lifetime of friendship, superior leadership, and support.

My intense gratitude extends to everyone who has ever served and sacrificed as part of the fighting team of the American military, including my immediate brothers and sister, Steve, John, and Kathy, and everyone I consider a brother or sister because they wear or wore the uniform. I think military service is tough on parents, and, certainly, mine, Bob and Shirley Kelly, worried more than their fair share.

Finally, I am grateful for the yin to my yang, Randall Dawson, whose love, stability, and support provides me with grounding and reality.

Mary C. Kelly

For the past 25 years, we have been blessed with terrific partnerships with our many and diverse clients. We are grateful for the trust you put in our team. With each project, we learn from members of the management team and their employees. Without our clients who have implemented the recommendations we share in this book, we would not have witnessed, first-hand, the positive results that are achieved when great leaders have the desire to drive results and create a culture where employees love coming to work.

I could not do what I love to do every day without the support of Kathleen, my wife, and my three children, Barron, Brooke and Brianne. Thank you for always being a source of encouragement and inspiration, and never once asking, "Daddy, why do you travel so much?" You inspire me to do great work!

Last, this book is for my dad, who was the wisest man I knew. He would have been 95 years old this year, and he spent the last six months of his life fighting the hard fight of losing his memory and losing all ability to make decisions for himself. Dad went to Heaven on August 18, 2015. Of the eleven books we have written, this is the only one on which Dad did not do the first proof. If you find a grammatical error, know that my Dad would have been on it. It was an honor to give help each day to a dad who spent his whole life giving to me, our family, and many others, never once asking for help in return.

Peter B. Stark

Working together on this book helped us become better leaders and made this book project a lot more fun. We truly are better when we work together.

Table of Contents

Introduction 1

1 | They Lack a Compelling Vision and Clear Goals 5

2 | They Torpedo Trust. 27

3 | They Just Don't Care! 51

4 | They are Unfair 71

5 | They Don't Understand We Are One Team. 91

6 | They Want To Be Miss Congeniality. 113

7 | Their Confidence Becomes Arrogance. 129

Conclusion. 143

The 7 Ways to Engage. 153

Appendix. 157

Introduction

Over the past twenty years, we have had the privilege of working with thousands of managers in corporate, military, and nonprofit environments. In our roles as leaders, consultants, speakers, and authors, we witness firsthand the qualities that make a leader great. We have taught in universities, authored nineteen books, and published over 500 articles with the mission of helping managers acquire the skills necessary to succeed as leaders.

On the surface, becoming a great leader appears relatively simple. People are often told that anyone can be a leader, that everyone is, in fact, a leader, and that true leadership has nothing to do with an authoritative title.

We agree. We found an abundance of supervisors, military personnel, managers, vice presidents, and CEOs within organizations with positions of authority. These managers have a title that allows them to tell others what to do. They set the goals and directions and administer budgets. Ideally, they put the right people on the bus and align the organizational structure to effectively meet the goals. Yet, many managers successfully accomplish routine tasks (illustrated by their direct reports) and produce results for their organizations, but they fail to become truly effective and inspiring leaders.

The defining factor of a strong leader is rooted in the relationships they build with their followers and how effectively they propel the organization toward great achievement. Becoming a great leader and earning relationships with people who are motivated to follow you for long periods of time *is hard work.* If it were easy, there would be an abundance of great leaders. All companies would flourish, and all employees would be excited to come to work. And we, as executive consultants, would be unemployed.

To be clear, managers manage projects and things while leaders lead and inspire people. We know there are people in managerial positions who are both managers and leaders, and then there are people who are neither. Our focus in this book is to inspire people who want to lead others to success and to provide the tools to accomplish that.

Why Leaders Fail and the 7 Prescriptions for Success addresses why so many managers fail in their leadership roles. Through our research and executive coaching work with clients, we became aware of how many well-intentioned, really good professionals get promoted into leadership roles, and then fail. The stories and examples in *Why Leaders Fail ...* are real-life examples we have encountered in our careers. Some are success stories in which managers corrected their undermining behaviors, developed new skills, and built the skills and networks of a great leader. Other examples are less positive with managers failing to correct their negative behaviors, and, eventually, losing their jobs as a result.

Each chapter focuses on a specific behavior or deficiency that undermines a manager's ability to lead and causes them to derail from their track to leadership success. Each chapter also outlines a Prescription for Success, followed by 7 Tips for Success that all aspiring leaders can put into action today. We hope that our research will not only pinpoint why leaders fail, but also provide inspiration and guidance to help more managers become great leaders.

Bonus! This book provides you with access to a free, online mini-version of the Peter Barron Stark Companies Leadership Development Assessment. The assessment is specifically adapted to measure the skills provided in this book. Upon completion, you will be able to compare your results to our two different leadership benchmarks. This provides a metric for you to identify areas of effectiveness as well as opportunities for improvement.

Plus, there are links throughout the book that guide readers to additional tools for success. Mary and the Productive Leaders team developed a 5-Minute Success Series that gives leaders templates for topics many leaders struggle with, such as creating a vision, strategic planning, productivity, and social media.

As you start reading this book, you will notice that we use the terms *manager* and *leader* interchangeably. However, we recognize and describe the significant differences between a manager and a leader throughout the book. Our goal is that *managers* will utilize the skills we prescribe to ultimately become effective *leaders*.

As we share our ideas with you, it is important to see this book for what it is: insight from two consultants on the skills needed to be a great leader. We are the first to acknowledge that our recommendations will not work in every situation. Leaders need to adapt the material for their unique needs and situations. You may have to call in a coach or other expert.

At the same time, we are also convinced that, if managers and supervisors apply the skills we describe, they will eliminate about 90% of the executive coaching work done in most organizations!

The skills presented here work. If you are willing to invest the time to read, learn, take the assessment, and practice these skills on the job, you will be proud of the results. You and your employees will accomplish more, and everyone will gain more enjoyment from working together. We wish you great success!

1

They Lack a Compelling Vision and Clear Goals

The very essence of leadership is [that] you have a vision. It's got to be a vision you articulate clearly and forcefully on every occasion. You can't blow an uncertain trumpet.

—Theodore Hesburgh

What is your vision for your team? Where do you see your team or organization in five years?

We asked a manager who was struggling with significant turnover and chaos in his department about his vision and goals. The manager responded, "I think your questions about my vision are management consultant garbage. My vision is not at the root of our team's problems." We then asked this manager what he thought the problem was, what the issues were, and where he was leading his department. He replied, "The high turnover will continue until Human Resources hires better employees."

Instead of taking responsibility for the leadership problem and articulating a clear and compelling vision for the future of his department, this manager blamed his failures on another department within the organization.

Another manager received the results of her individual 360°
Leadership Development Assessment feedback and asserted,
"I get the vision thing." When prompted for an explanation,
this leader explained that she had previously tried to put
into practice what she had learned in leadership training but
realized that, while she was focused on getting the operational tasks done right on a daily basis, she lacked a bigger
picture to steer the course.

She cheerfully admitted that the way she got things done
when faced with a challenge involved "setting my hair on
fire and jumping up and down on a table to get people to
sit up and take notice." She "managed" by initiating crises
and uncertainty instead of leading with a vision, clear
goals, and clear direction. She ultimately realized that she
needed a strategic picture for the long term.

Though their reactions to their predicaments were quite
different, these leaders were faced with the same obstacle:
they lacked both a mission and a compelling positive vision
for themselves and their teams.

Why do we need vision? Is it not enough to show up for work,
do what we are paid to do, and go home? Why do we need more?

First, **a vision instills a sense of purpose.** People need to
know where the team or organization is going and why they
are working so hard to get there. Employees need to believe
that what they contribute is important, and that they are
part of a cause larger than themselves.

Second, **a vision keeps us on track.** By giving us a big picture
of where we are going, a vision reaffirms our path and gives
us a reason to continue when we encounter obstacles and
challenges along the way.

Finally, **a vision guides communication, decisions, and feedback between managers and employees.** People do not quit their jobs. People quit managers who lack a positive vision of their future. Employees leave because they do not feel valued or appreciated, or they feel that what they do doesn't matter. Their managers frequently fail to consider employee feedback because the managers themselves are not sure where they are heading. They cannot connect the employees' feedback and suggestions to a clear vision and goals. As a result, these supervisors habitually ignore feedback instead of acting on it or responding to it. When employees' suggestions for improvement are ignored, employees become discouraged and the leadership development process is delayed.

In reality, there's never time in your busy routine to think about developing a vision. Just putting out the day-to-day fires you encounter in your supervisory role is a full-time job and can consume your entire day. However, if you find yourself feeling frustrated, running short on patience, and worrying about overreacting to a situation at the end of a challenging day, it is time to make developing your leadership vision a priority. Creating a compelling vision is one of the most valuable strategies a leader can create for both themselves and their team. There is no better time than now to either review and update your existing leadership vision, or take the time to craft your first leadership vision. Involve your team in crafting a vision; this makes it their vision as well.

Great visions help leaders succeed for the following reasons:
- Concentrate everyone's focus and energy toward a common goal.
- Build teamwork by inspiring excitement about the future.
- Build momentum to overcome problems that develop.
- Provide motivation for and belief in the larger cause.
- Transcend pettiness.

Every Leader Needs a Great Vision

A vision is clear mental picture of a future desired state, preferably written down and communicated clearly and often.

We are not big fans of jigsaw puzzles. Peter once worked on one for over three hours and found a not-so-encouraging five out of 2000 pieces that fit together. He glanced over at the picture on the box-top, and wondered, "Why am I duplicating this effort? I know exactly what the end result will be, I have it right here on the box."

While, for some of us, it may be a dubious hobby, a 2000-piece jigsaw puzzle offers a great analogy for a vision. Specifically, the picture on the puzzle box is your vision. It is extremely difficult to complete a jigsaw puzzle without having that picture to reference, and the same is true for realizing your vision.

Before you begin organizing and assembling the small puzzle pieces that are inside the box, the picture on top very clearly reflects the final result. It shows you what you are trying to build. That is your vision—the outcome you're striving to create.

It is important to align your personal vision with the vision of the organization. When the vision you create and communicate to your employees shows a clear connection to the vision of the organization, your team understands the purpose of what they are doing, and how their contributions are valuable to the realization of both the team's and the organization's visions.

Visions should be clear, concise, and compelling. They should outline where you want to be. Consider these examples:

Our vision is to be earth's most customer centric company; to build a place where people can come to find and discover anything they might want to buy online.

—Amazon

Create a better everyday life for the many people.

—IKEA

For us at Patagonia, a love of wild and beautiful places demands participation in the fight to save them, and to help reverse the steep decline in the overall environmental health of our planet.

—Patagonia

People often confuse a mission with a vision. A mission represents what we do, and it often involves our customers. Consider these examples of missions:

To organize the world's information and make it universally accessible and useful.

—Google

Provide a global trading platform where practically anyone can trade practically anything.

—eBay

To bring inspiration and innovation to every athlete in the world.

—Nike

To meet the goal of clearly communicating both the purpose and the outcome they are striving to create, some organizations utilize a mission and vision combination, such as:

*Our mission is to inspire and nurture the human spirit
—one person, one cup and one neighborhood at a time.*

—Starbucks

We will provide branded products and services of superior quality and value that improve the lives of the world's consumers. As a result, consumers will reward us with leadership sales profit and value creation, allowing our people or shareholders and the communities in which we live and work to prosper.

—Proctor and Gamble

Although many organizations combine their mission and vision in one statement, there is a difference. A mission statement describes what business you are in and who your customers are. A vision describes how you will operate and what actions you will take to accomplish the vision. Although every Catholic Church in the world has the same mission that is handed to them by the Vatican, every Catholic parish has a different vision of how they will execute the mission. Some churches, for instance, will have schools on site, while other parishes will focus their vision on serving the needs of the senior populations or the poor and needy.

There Are Three Types of Visions

If you, as the leader, do not set the tone and provide your team with a compelling positive vision, people will end up defaulting into one of two other vision types: status quo visions and negative visions.

Positive Visions

Leaders who communicate a positive vision believe that today is great and tomorrow will be even better. They believe that problems are opportunities and that people are capable of achieving the impossible. Leaders with positive visions truly believe in, and are committed to, the possibilities.

Only real, inspirational visions have the power to raise morale to an even higher level. Tim Cook, Apple's CEO, demonstrated the impact of a powerful vision during an employee memorial service for Steve Jobs. In a time of great uncertainty and enormous expectations, he stood up and told all the gathered employees, "Our best days are ahead of us." It was both an incredibly difficult and powerful message to deliver, considering the circumstances.

If you, as a leader, do not have your own positive vision, remember: "You're going to be dead for a lot longer than you're alive." You do not have time to waste on visions that do not benefit you.

Status Quo Visions

We once interviewed a manager who was the perfect embodiment of a status quo vision. He was working for the federal government and only a couple of years away from retirement. He told us "I just want to hang on and do what I have to do for two more years." He was reporting to a new boss, and he was unhappy with the disruption of his status quo vision. "I just want to tell this new guy, 'Look, my old boss left me alone and didn't

If you, as the leader, do not set the tone and provide your team with a compelling positive vision, people will end up defaulting into one of two other vision types: status quo visions and negative visions.

bug me or ask me to change the way I do things. This suited me just fine, and we got along without any issues. Please don't ask me to change what I've been doing when I'm two years away from being done.'"

His status quo vision is all too common among people who do not care very much about their jobs or the people they work with. They show up, do the minimum amount of work it takes to be largely left alone, and collect their paycheck.

The challenge with status quo visionaries is that they do not allow for forward movement; you essentially stand still. When your customers and competitors keep raising the bar and turning their strategic visions into action, you and your organization are no longer just standing still, you are effectively moving backwards.

Negative Visions

These people hate everything and almost everyone. They hate their job, their boss, their desk, their customers, and they make sure to let everyone around them know. They look at you and say "You think today is bad? Just wait! It's going to get worse." For them, it does. They truly believe tomorrow is going to be worse than today.

The biggest problem with these negative visionaries is that they stick with you and your organization for a lifetime. You might wonder "Why? If they don't like me, they don't like the boss, and they don't like our company, why don't they just leave?"

There are two very good reasons why these people won't leave.

1) They have zero options. Anyone who has had to work with them and their negativity certainly will not bring them along

when they take a job elsewhere nor can they recommend them to someone else.

2) As miserable as they may be currently, their vision of a change is even more dire. They truly believe that their next boss, department, or company could be worse than this one. They know the grass is not always greener on the other side of the fence. In fact, they anticipate the grass will probably grow higher and require more mowing. Why would they leave their current situation for one with the potential of more work and higher performance standards? Negative people also know that a new boss will not put up with their negative vision, attitude, and behaviors.

As much as you wish the negative people would just leave, they fully intend to stay with your organization, spreading their ill will and discontent as far as they can.

Negative managers are some of the greatest visionaries of all time. Their visions are self-perpetuating because they expect poor outcomes. They are committed to their negative vision and often, either deliberately or subconsciously, take actions that turn their vision into reality.

If the vision is so important, why don't more leaders create one? We hear many excuses, but these are the ones we hear most often:

- I don't have time; I'm too busy getting the job done.
- It's my manager's job to tell me what the vision is.
- No one ever pays attention to a vision after it's created.
- It doesn't matter what we suggest or come up with, senior leaders won't support it anyway.

Creating a Vision is Hard Work!

One excuse we rarely hear from managers is that collaborating with the team to create a compelling, positive vision is hard work. To start with a blank sheet of paper and lead a group to a shared vision that is truly aspirational is one of the most difficult tasks a leader can accomplish. It is, however, one of the most important accomplishments of leadership. When it is done right, the time invested in crafting your vision is well worth it.

As with anything that requires collaborative work, crafting a compelling positive vision is a task managers find easy to procrastinate. If given the choice between doing an operational task on the always growing "things to do" list or completing a strategic task that will bring long-term value to the team, most managers will do the operational tasks first. Why? It is not easy to articulate a vision when working by yourself. It takes thought, discussion, and consideration. Creating a vision that is inspiring, valuable, and long-lasting is an involved process that most people are not taught. In many cases, it is also tough to see the immediate benefit of the task. The most difficult step is often the first one: to sit down and think, and then put your thoughts on paper. It is even more difficult to involve a team in the development of a vision and bring that team to a consensus.

The manager who led her team by "setting her hair on fire" finally laughed when she realized what she was doing. She said she was starting to understand the important role a positive vision would play in defining who she wanted to become as a leader, what she wanted to create for her team, and where she wanted to take her division.

She talked about the quiet, reflective time it took to explore ideas about who she was as a manager, and who she wanted to become as a leader. She readily admitted that crafting the vision was a struggle, and she was worried that this process would absorb time that she did not have. When she realized what could happen if she had the right vision, she was determined to make the time to accomplish the task. She concluded by sharing that she thought this was the missing piece that was going to help her make sense of all the leadership training her company had provided her with over the past few years.

Prescription for Vision Success

Great leaders understand the value and benefits of a positive vision. They make the time to develop and communicate their vision and take the needed actions to turn that vision into a reality.

Know the Why

As a leader, you need to engage other people with an idea, a goal, and the jigsaw puzzle box picture that clearly communicates what you are trying to achieve. People need to know what they are doing and why.

Real commitment is rooted in knowing why you are assembling the jigsaw puzzle. If you know you will spray shellac on the completed puzzle and frame it to display in the dining room, then you are motivated to keep going even when all 500 of the landscape pieces appear to be the exact same shade of green.

Simon Sinek startled some business leaders with his book, *Start with Why: How Great Leaders Inspire Everyone to Take Action*, when he described the importance of employees knowing why they do what they do. Sinek explains that the business of creating products may be easily replicated and commoditized. However, if the leadership is strong and people understand their vision, then no other business can compete with the level of loyalty, focus, and experience you have at your disposal.

Know the why. If you are assembling the puzzle just so you can dump the puzzle pieces back into the box after it is completed, then you have created busy work for yourself and those around you. People think, and rightly so, "Why bother? This doesn't matter and is a waste of time." When people do not understand why what they are doing matters, the motivation to keep going dies.

Some people think visions are only for corporations, but organizations of all sizes and missions need vision.

Since Pope Francis was elected by his fellow cardinals in March 2013, his leadership and vision for the world have propelled his influence, even among non-Catholics. He is a spiritual rock star. He's appeared on the covers of *Time* magazine, *National Geographic*, and *Rolling Stone.* Pope John Paul II and Benedict XVI, Pope Francis' predecessors, both had visions with similar themes, yet lacked Pope Francis' attention and impact on the world.

As a leader, what is it about Pope Francis that attracts millions of people who want to follow him and hear his ideas for the future of our world? His message of inclusivity, caring for others, compassion, and humility is so powerful that it extends to non-Catholics, non-Christians, and even nonbelievers.

Although the Pope has many components to his vision, there are two big pieces of his puzzle, in particular, that are worth pointing out. First is his vision of spreading God's mercy and extending God's compassion for the poor and oppressed through the Church. The second big piece of the Pope's vision puzzle is his plan to turn the Vatican into a global model of best practices in financial administration. Wow! Pope Francis is the CEO of an organization that has been plagued by corruption, arrogance, financial chaos, and the criminal abuse of both children and adults. To turn the Vatican and Church into a global model of best practices is a huge vision ... one that Pope Francis' believers want to buy into.

Ask the Right Questions

Great visions address the following types of questions:

- What picture do we want to create for the future of the organization?
- What legacy are we leaving for future leaders?
- How do we want to be seen in 3, 5, 10, and 50 years by our employees?
  By our customers?
  By our community?
- What is the larger cause?
- What is our higher purpose?

Aim High

The vision should be big, really big. Almost impossible. It needs to be strong enough to guide your team or organization for the next 3, 5, or 10 years. Your vision should be:

- Exciting and compelling;
- A force that encourages and energizes everyone involved;
- A picture of what the organization hopes to achieve;
- Idealistic: don't limit yourself to what you think can "realistically" happen; shoot for the moon, figuratively (the realistic aspects will follow);
- Not time-bound: in 5 to 10 years, you may still not have achieved your vision, and that is okay.

Follow the Six Steps to Building Your Vision

Thankfully, you get to create the vision that guides your path. Your vision may have nothing to do with the reality of today, and everything to do with the outcome you want to create for your organization or team in the future.

Creating a lasting, meaningful vision requires the following six steps. Trying to shortcut these steps diminishes the value, longevity, and success of the vision.

 Step One: Create an Image of the Vision

To start the visioning process, get in touch with your true intentions and resolutions. What is important to you? What matters? What do you care passionately about? What do you really want to achieve? If resources were not a constraint, what would you set out to do?

The visioning process requires quiet reflection. Step back from your busy, fast-paced environment and relax. If you are working on a vision for your team, you and your team may need to take a day or two away from the office. Envisioning requires imagery and creativity. The more relaxed you are and the farther away you are from day-to-day tensions, the easier it is to create and visualize. A vision comes from the heart, and it must be truly meaningful to you and those around you. Create a mental picture, described in words, of what you want.

Many people have a difficult time creating a vision because that vision may be so far removed from reality. Yet, it is that very distance or gap between the vision and current reality that propels you toward achievement.

> *It is the distance or gap between the vision and current reality that propels you toward achievement.*

This concept was first described by Robert Fritz in his book, *The Path of Least Resistance.* Fritz calls it structural tension. There are two components to structural tension. The first component is the *vision*, or the picture, of what you want. The second component is the *current reality*, or what you have now. As Fritz maintains, the discrepancy between what you have (current reality) and the result you want (vision) creates structural tension. This tension helps you create the motivation and passion to do what you need to do to close the gap between your current reality and your future vision.

Structural tension is useful because it seeks resolution. In other words, to resolve the tension between your vision and current reality, one or the other has to give. As Fritz describes:

> Structural tension may be resolved in one of two ways. Resolve it through a change in current reality so your outward circumstances correspond more closely with your vision. On the other hand, the tension may be resolved through a change in your vision, so you alter the result you want to correspond more closely with what you have now.

To achieve what you really want, crystallize the vision. Make it real and believe it, in both your mind and in your heart. Then, acknowledge the current reality. Feel the tension between the two, and allow that structural tension to propel you towards your vision and what you truly want.

 Step Two: Decide on Actions

Now that the vision is clear, you can begin to determine the actions that must be taken to achieve the vision. These actions become the specific goals that are to be accomplished. A goal is a target, an end, or an objective with a schedule and a deadline. Accomplishing these targets—or goals—brings you closer to your vision.

For example, if your personal vision is to achieve a more prominent position in your organization or to move higher up on your career ladder, you would first go through the visioning process and become crystal clear on what it is you actually want.

You want to be the CEO. You know exactly what that job looks like and how it feels. Then ask, "What do I need to accomplish to get to my vision?" One action may be to go back to school and complete the advanced business degree needed for that position. If you need the degree to achieve the vision, it becomes one of your key goals.

At this point in the goal-setting process, list the various actions you must take to achieve your vision. You will have both short-term and long-term goals, and both are important. As we move through the next steps, we will discuss how to write effective goal statements.

Every leader needs to be clear on their organizational and

personal leadership vision. In the military, this is called a commander's intent.

 ### Step Three: Identify Roadblocks

After you identify the vision and the key actions or goals necessary to achieve it, you can proactively identify the barriers or roadblocks that may get in your way.

It may sound negative to spend time and energy thinking about obstructions or problems, but there are two good reasons for this step.

First, if you are able to analyze the problems that could stop you, you can begin to generate proactive plans to navigate around the problems if they arise. And second, when barriers do pop up, they will not stop the forward momentum because you have a plan of action ready to go.

Many people have their goals undermined when problems surface. They reach a roadblock and become paralyzed because they did not consider the difficulty of the situation. As soon as obstacles occur, the negative people on your team will take this opportunity to remind you that they warned you about the problems and that your vision is doomed. Unfortunately for you, these negative people secretly enjoy watching others run into problems.

Maybe one of your goals is to go back to school and get your degree. Some of the roadblocks you could anticipate might include

- Not having enough time to study and attend classes;
- A fear of going back to being a student;
- Financial constraints.

For each of the roadblocks you identify, develop strategies to navigate around the problems. These may include changing your own thinking and being open to accepting help from others. You might need to set aside specific time blocks to do what you need to do. Maybe you need to take out a student loan. If you keep your vision in mind as you move forward, overcoming the roadblocks will not be as tough.

 Step Four: List the Benefits

What does achieving your vision do for you? After you have listed the problems, it is much easier to generate a list of the benefits you will receive when you achieve your goal. The question that needs to be answered is "Do the benefits make the goal worth achieving?" If the answer is yes, you know that tackling the problems is worth it to achieve the benefits of goal attainment. Having the benefits outlined helps during those moments of doubt, or when the end goal seems far away.

Continuing with our example, some of the benefits of going back to school and obtaining a degree might be:

- Improved chances for promotion;
- Increased salary;
- Enhanced self-esteem;
- Serving as a role model for your children;
- The feeling of accomplishing something you have wanted for many years.

As you list the benefits, make sure the benefits outweigh the problems you will encounter. If the benefits do not outweigh the problems, the problems will stop you. Focus on the benefits. They will help you get through the tough times.

Step Five: Write the Goal

Your vision is a goal. Research done on high achievers shows that successful goal setters write out their goals, as well as the steps needed to achieve them. There is something powerful and almost magical about writing down goals. If the goal is not written, it is merely an idea or a wish. Writing down your goal makes it a commitment and brings it to life.

Your goals should be broken down into smaller daily, weekly, or monthly goals to help keep you on track. When they are completed, post your goals and steps where you can see them. When your goals are written down and visible, you subconsciously start working on them. It is okay to re-evaluate your goals along the way toward achieving your vision. Goals may evolve as technology and industry changes. When you reach a significant goal, take time to celebrate the success.

You may, at some point, have come across the **S-M-A-R-T** model for articulating goals.

Each letter of the **S-M-A-R-T** model refers to a characteristic of effective goals.

S pecific

M easurable

A ttainable

R elevant

T ime bound

Specific. Good goals are specific, and detail exactly what is to be accomplished. Do not be vague or general. For example, a business goal to "increase profits" is not enough. A SMART goal would be phrased "Gain one new client per month for the next two years."

Measurable. You must be able to measure the success of your goal. In other words, how will you know when you are successful? Whether the goal is broken down into number of units produced, salary earned, days worked, pounds lost, chapters completed, or number of classes attended, you need a way to quantify your results. Measuring your results helps to keep you moving toward your goal. Yes, it is a great motivator!

Attainable. Research shows that high achievers set goals that challenge their abilities but are not unrealistically out of reach. When you set challenging but attainable goals, you experience success and increase your self-esteem. Be realistic about your goals. It is not unrealistic to go back to school for a degree. It is unrealistic to expect to get a doctorate in only one year. Make your goals challenging, but keep them realistic. You need to be able to picture a positive outcome.

Relevant. Do not forget that your vision is the driver for your goals. Make sure that your goals are relevant to the vision. The accomplishment of each goal should move you closer to the realization of your vision.

Time bound. Good goals have a time frame. When you set a specific time frame to get something done, you are able to ensure it will take you that amount of time (or even less time) to complete the task than if you had no time frame at all.

One example of this is when you prepare to travel or go on vacation. You have all sorts of tasks that need to be accomplished before you leave. You may be rushed, but you will always get the tasks done. You have to, because you are leaving. If there were no looming deadline, those same tasks would most likely take you two or three times as long to accomplish. Life is short! Set a time frame. You will always accomplish more that way.

What types of goals do great leaders set? Great leaders set ambitious goals for individuals and their team. Ambitious goals that push team members work well for two reasons. First, there is nothing motivating about setting a mediocre or low goal and achieving it. Second, even if the ambitious goal is not reached, the team will still be farther along than it would be if a low goal had been set and reached.

 Step Six: Design an Action Plan

Now that you have your intentions—you know exactly what you want to achieve and by when—it is time to design a specific action plan to achieve the goals. This is a step-by-step breakdown of the small actions you will take to achieve each goal and when you will take them.

Every time you complete an action, check it off, and celebrate. You are on your way to achieving your ultimate goal!

Remember, the secret to achieving goals is your willingness to make sacrifices and do whatever it takes to get there. It means you are willing to confront problems and roadblocks, and work around them. It means you will write out your goals and ensure they are **S-M-A-R-T**. It takes work. And it also means you will reap the benefits of bringing your vision to life.

A great vision, combined with the short- and long-term

goals necessary to turn that vision into a reality, is a key to great leadership. With a powerful positive vision, most team members will find it easier to feel excitement and pride in the work they do.

Great leaders create a positive vision and set a course of action. They expect to see their vision become a reality. They also expect to *enjoy* the challenges, frustrations, personal and professional development, and learning opportunities that come with thinking big and achieving big.

> *Vision without action is merely a dream. Action without vision just passes the time. Vision with action can change the world.*
>
> —Joel A. Barker, futurist, author, and filmmaker

7 Tips for Creating a Compelling Vision

1. Make sure the vision is compelling, ambitious, aspirational, and clearly defined.

2. Know the *Why*.

3. The *mission* is what you do. The *vision* is the image of where you are going.

4. Great visions focus teams toward a common goal. They need to be big enough to create dynamic tension.

5. Make sure everyone in the organization is clear on their role in fulfilling the vision.

6. Understand that working toward a powerful vision means pushing beyond the status quo.

7. Great leaders transform vision into smart goals and celebrate achievements.

2

They Torpedo Trust

If you don't have trust inside your company, then you can't transfer it to your customers.

—Roger Staubach

Trust is a critical element in the workplace. People have to trust each other on both big and small issues. Seemingly harmless requests or actions that undermine trust can have big consequences.

In a coaching engagement, we worked with a seasoned mid-level manager who was great with her people and respected by her bosses. She consistently came in under budget and delivered her projects ahead of schedule. She was focused, productive, and energetic.

This manager's team morale was high, and direct reports responded well to her leadership. Everyone seemed happy. From the outside, it appeared to be a perfect work environment. In our coaching, however, we encountered a huge problem; this manager did not trust her direct supervisor.

Why? Her direct supervisor had asked her to lie to his boss

about his whereabouts. Her direct supervisor wanted his boss to think he was working harder than he actually was. He asked her to lie and say he was in meetings with clients when he was at the gym, at home for a long lunch, or golfing. At first, it was once or twice a month. Then it became once or twice a week.

This manager was put in an uncomfortable and untenable position. She wanted to focus on doing a good job for her boss and the organization, but she did not want to compromise her integrity by lying. She tried to cover for her boss as much as possible without outright lying, but the day came when the CEO cornered her and she told the truth. She was not sure how the conversation between the two leaders ensued, but her working relationship with both leaders was compromised. The CEO did not communicate back to this manager to assure her she did the right thing. Instead, she was reprimanded and blamed by her direct supervisor for telling the truth.

The direct supervisor's boss no longer trusted the department, and support for that department quickly went downhill. Profit margins decreased. The talented manager found another job. The lying senior manager continued to lose good direct reports and his engagement scores continued in a downward spiral until he was fired.

Little lies can lead to big problems, and, as shown below, lies are not the only behaviors that lead to mistrust in relationships. Trust is a necessary factor in the workplace, and great leaders work hard to earn, and keep, the trust and confidence of their employees.

Why Trust at Work Matters

Why does it matter if employees trust their managers? When people do not trust their leaders, they are much more likely to leave their positions if the option is available to them. If you are in a leadership position and have a high rate of turnover among employees, one of the issues at play may be a lack of trust.

When we compare the survey results of the Best of the Best organizations to the Overall Benchmark organizations in our research, the Best of the Best employees rate their senior leaders 22.0 percentage points higher at being committed to building trust with employees. Employees at the Best of the Best organizations also trust the decisions of senior leaders at a higher rate than average employees.[1]

What undermines trust? It is a hard question to ask. It is an even harder question to get an honest answer to when you are the person in charge. We surveyed 75 junior military officers and asked them what their leaders do that cause them to lose trust. The most frequently stated answers are consistent with the reasons civilian employees give for not trusting their corporate business leaders.

Lying, not telling the whole story, or clouding intent topped the list. Most employees consider leaders lying to their people to be the equivalent of a mortal sin; it is virtually impossible to recover from. Other reasons the junior officers mentioned included:

- lack of transparency,
- acting or speaking disrespectfully,
- withholding information,
- creating uncertainty,
- stealing,

[1] Peter Barron Stark Companies has two benchmarks for organizations to compare their survey results against. The Best-of-the-Best Benchmark includes the top quarter of organizations surveyed, while the Overall Benchmark includes all companies surveyed. Learn more about our benchmarks at http://bit.ly/1RT3WQd

- not trusting subordinates,
- unethical enforcement,
- setting unattainable standards,
- gossiping or talking about other team members behind their backs,
- disloyalty and a lack of support for subordinates, and
- acting selfishly.

Path to Failure

Let's look at some of these issues and other transgressions that can undermine trust.

Lying

Nothing destroys the faith and confidence of people working in an organization faster than finding out their direct supervisor lied to them. It does not have to be a big lie. A small, seemingly inconsequential lie can have a huge impact on an employee's level of trust in a leader. If their leader is willing to lie to them about little things of little consequence, what prevents them from lying to them about matters of real importance?

> Nothing destroys the faith and confidence of people working in an organization faster than finding out their direct supervisor lied to them.

Lying by Omission

Telling the truth, the whole truth, and nothing but the truth seems like a good idea. So why is it so hard for leaders in organizations to tell the whole truth? Oftentimes, it is not that easy. Leaders often only have partial information themselves, or they provide information that is later contradicted by updated information. Therefore, many leaders are in the habit of not conveying information until it can be verified multiple times. The problem with that delay is it creates uncertainty for the other team members. Every time employees feel uncertain about their future with the company, product issues, or personnel changes, it causes a loss of productivity and feeds mistrust.

Some leaders are also slow to realize that employees often find information faster than the hierarchy can promulgate it. This leaves leaders in the unenviable position of not sharing official information because they do not have it. By the time a leader lets people know what he knows, they have already received that information, and more.

Certain levels of leadership may also be restricted with regards to how much information they are allowed to provide their employees. In those instances, they need to be honest and let their employees know what they can provide and what they cannot provide. Employees will understand if the circumstances are adequately communicated.

Lacking Clear Communication

Imagine you are working at a job you love, in an organization you enjoy, for a manager you like. You have the education, technical knowledge, and real life experience that allow you to excel at this job. You have years of experience working as a successful manager, and you have an excellent reputation as a forward-thinking leader in both your organization and your industry. Then, you get a new supervisor.

Your new boss does not know you or anyone else. He asks lots of questions every time you make a decision. He wants to know details that are far below his paygrade, requiring you to spend a substantial amount of time responding to his seemingly endless queries for information.

You move some people around projects, and your new boss wants to know why. You let one employee leave early on Monday because they worked late last week, and your new boss wants to know why. It feels as if every decision you make is being questioned. You feel your authority is being undermined and your direct reports have started to challenge your decisions. You suddenly believe your boss does not trust you to run your team.

You stop functioning as an effective leader. You think, "If my manager doesn't trust me, why should I try?" "If everything I do is being questioned, it's easier to not do anything." You start to lose confidence and it feels like you cannot do anything right. You feel micromanaged to the point where you are afraid to make decisions. You stop trying.

Now, look at this scenario from the boss' perspective.

You have just taken on a new, high-profile job. You want to learn everything you can about the people and the systems you have in place. You have read *The Competent Leader* and *Master Your World*. You ask a lot of questions and you listen carefully to the answers.

The more you show interest in your direct reports and what they do, however, the more they seem to push back and resist you as their new manager. You wonder if maybe they do not like you. You wonder if they do not trust or respect you. You wonder if their loyalty to the old boss is so strong they will never accept you or the changes you want to make in their department. You wonder whether or not they are going to get onboard with your vision. You worry that, if things do not improve, you might have to let some people go. Someone once told you, "This is not truly your team unless you have personally hired everyone here." You are starting to think that may be true.

This example involves two great workers and leaders with aligned visions and a shared work ethic. Yet, a lack of direct, honest, and timely communication among both team members leads to micro-management and a massive breakdown of trust.

Disrespecting Others' Time

We coached one of the two top leaders at a prestigious technology company. This leader was admired by his boss, his peers, and his employees. A 360° Leadership Development Assessment indicated that literally everyone in the organization respected and genuinely liked him. This leader possessed many of the qualities of a great leader. He genuinely cared about his people, listened well, and was not afraid to make tough decisions. He scored high on our assessments.

However, there was one overarching problem that *every single person* mentioned about this particular leader. He was always late—to meetings, appointments with his team, and even when addressing his entire company!

He often kept subordinates waiting for 10, 20, or 45 minutes while he finished up with other people. The number one problem resulting from this was direct reports feeling disrespected by his broken time promises. Trust broke down because this leader consistently failed to fulfill his commitments.

This was not a rare occurrence; it happened every day. He promised to be in a certain location at a certain time, and then broke that promise. Each day that he failed to follow through on his promises, they trusted him a little less, until they finally gave up on him ever being where he was supposed to be. Not only did he inconvenience other people, but he was incredibly disrespectful of their time.

This sounds like a small issue, but his failure to meet with people or attend meetings when he said he would led to diminished trust among employees, and increased doubt about his other abilities.

Withholding Information

Some leaders we work with defend their lack of communication by saying they are too busy or that the timing is not right. With a little more time, leaders feel they will have more accurate information or their employees will be better prepared to receive the information. What these leaders fail to understand is that their efforts to try to get the right information to their people at the right time most often results in the information being delivered too late. Employees have already learned the information through their coworkers, the media, or on social media. When the information does not come directly from their manager, employees lose trust in their leaders. It appears as though the leader did not know what was going on or they did not care enough about the employees to get them the needed information in a timely manner.

> *I'd rather have 90% of the information now than 100% in six months.*
>
> —Lt. Gen. Harold T. Fields, U.S. Army (ret)

It is better to be transparent, providing full disclosure with what you know than to wait until you have 100 percent of the information. Chances are extremely high you will never have 100 percent of the information.

Creating uncertainty about the future

A CEO announced to the entire company, "We haven't decided who will stay and who will be laid off yet." This CEO went on to add, "We recently conducted evaluations and are doing extensive analysis. We'll announce the results of our findings in two to three weeks." The CEO's intentions were good. She tried to convey confidence to the employees that the process they were using to determine who would stay and who would go was thorough, comprehensive, and well thought out.

The problem was that some of those employees had already been told they would be leaving. Naturally, they felt no reason not to share this information with their current co-workers. Team members felt their leadership team was lying to them ... and they were!

Information now travels faster than ever. Leaders have to make sure they stay ahead of their organization's pipeline, and they have to get information out as quickly as possible. Leaders need to understand that not conveying information in a direct, honest, and timely manner leads to their people feeling betrayed. When managers do not communicate, team members feel their leaders do not trust them with information. As a result, they do not share information with their leaders, and trust breaks down.

Stealing

When millennials in a recent survey cited stealing as a factor that eroded trust, we were initially dumbfounded. Did they really mean stealing? Were they really referring to taking the company's money or property and using it for personal use? Apparently, yes! One employee shared with us how she was required to complete her manager's expense report, which included personal travel expenses that were unrelated to the business. Enough said!

Demanding Face Time

Focusing on face time instead of results by demanding that employees adhere to specific working hours is a great way to both demotivate a highly engaged employee and demonstrate you do not trust them.

For many jobs, such as those in the restaurant or retail industry, specific working hours are a necessity. But for many salaried employees, accounting for their working hours seem denigrating. We all know people who show up at work and spend several hours not really working. There is very little a manager can do to ensure that every employee is contributing 100 percent of energy and potential at all times. Highly motivated people, however, are much more focused on the work they are doing as opposed to the hours spent working. If they are excited about the work, they will work until the job is done, even if that means taking the work home or working long hours.

At one technology development firm we watched a young manager kill the motivation of his team when he decided to impose strict working hours. He wanted everyone at work, at their desks, between 9:00 and 4:30, no exceptions.

His highly motivated employees interpreted that as:

- "You don't trust me, and you want to watch over my shoulder."
- "You want to micromanage me."
- "You don't know what I do, so you want to make sure whatever I am doing is done in the office."
- "You don't realize that where I generate revenue is in meetings with clients, and those take place outside this office."

Those same employees ended up leaving in disgust.

When you tell highly motivated and talented people "You must be in the office between 9:00 and 4:30," you are telling them you don't trust them. These employees realized the manager did not know what their roles entailed, and morale decreased even further. The attitude turned against the manager. Employees thought, "Okay, you want me to work between 9 and 4:30? Great. I will only work between 9 and 4:30. I'll show you."

Enforcing Rules Unethically

Hypocrisy (do as I say, not as I do) also triggers mistrust in employees. Expecting employees to adhere to all stated values and standards, but failing to adhere to those standards yourself, is guaranteed to decrease trust in both the leader and the organization.

One of the more entertaining (but oh so wrong!) examples occurred when the Army discovered soldiers were growing taller. As described in a white paper from the Army War College, *Lying to Ourselves*, a promotion board was looking through the evaluations of senior noncommissioned officers (NCOs). They discovered Army bosses were reporting soldiers at heights taller than they actually were to make sure that weight gains were kept within the Army's height/weight standards.

Employees trust leaders whose actions are consistent with what they say and how they hold themselves and others accountable. Employees believe what they see in the halls much more strongly than what they read on the walls or hear from their leaders.

> *Employees trust leaders whose actions are consistent with what they say and how they hold themselves and others accountable.*

Creating Unattainable Goals

Are you creating an environment in which it is virtually impossible for your people to succeed? We love a big, hairy, and audacious goal as much as the next person, and we love a good challenge. But if your goals are simply too challenging, you set your employees up for failure. Subordinates will examine what specific requirements need to be accomplished to meet the set standards and neglect the elements that are unlikely to be inspected. Goals need to be realistic so employees do not feel a need to falsify information to make it appear as though the goals are being met. If employees cannot trust their manager to set realistic and attainable goals, why should they trust them in other facets of their jobs?

Gossiping

When managers partake in gossip, employee trust is undermined for several reasons. First, most people walk away from the conversation, wondering "If this leader talks like this about others when they're not present, what are they saying about me when I'm not around?" Second, it communicates to others that the manager does not truly care about the people they are speaking negatively about. Employees do not trust managers who, they believe, do not care about their people.

Being Disloyal

The job of a leader is to serve and support the people who are on their team. This means that the needs of your employees and customers must come before your own. We worked with one manager who felt it was okay to publicly take sole credit for the work of his team. This manager loved the praise and recognition from others, but never passed it along or publicly recognized the great work of his team members. When managers are motivated by selfish gains and/or are primarily focused on promoting themselves, employees see right through that behavior and become mistrustful of their actions and intentions.

Breeding Mistrust

Mistrust breeds more mistrust, which results in uncertainty, disruption, blame, and anger. Enough mistrust can kill an organization. Managers who do not trust employees set up all sorts of safeguards to ensure their goals are met. For example, a manager may:

- Double- and triple-check an employee's work on the hunt for mistakes;
- Tell an employee not only *what* needs to be done, but exactly *how* to do it;
- Require employees to bring information to them so the manager can make the decision;
- Follow up excessively to ensure the work is being done the way the manager wants it completed;
- Request to be copied on all emails sent by the employee;
- Check in frequently to pinpoint the whereabouts of the employee.

Every one of these actions communicates to the employee they are not trusted. As a result, the employee starts to believe they cannot trust their manager. Both the manager and the employee then start taking actions that confirms each other's beliefs. Not feeling trusted, the employee stops trying at work. The employee refuses to make simple decisions because he or she strongly believes the manager will find errors with the work. The employee feels criticized and mistrusted so work output declines. In turn, the manager gets frustrated with the lack of work. Both wonder, "Why should I even try?"

Prescription for Trust Success

Whether you are a new or seasoned manager, building trust with your employees and your supervisor is critical to your ability to get things done. Do you have clout at work? Do your leaders? Clout is defined as the ability to influence others to get things done. Why do some people in organizations have clout and others do not? The answer often boils down to the level of trust others have in managers and their ability to get things done.

The following are proven behaviors and actions that will help you build trust with your supervisor and your employees:

Do What You Say You are Going to Do

This suggestion offers you the fastest path to trustworthiness. Do you follow through on what you say you are going to do? If you tell someone you are going to do something, write it down so you don't forget. Put it on your calendar or track it in an app. And then, do it. If you ask someone else to do something for you, write it down so you remember to check in with them to ensure its completion. This reinforces that the tasks you delegate are important.

Go Beyond the Conventional Relationship

As a manager, you are expected to fulfill your assigned responsibilities. Completing a performance appraisal is one of those responsibilities. Passing around a birthday card for everyone in the department to sign is not one of those responsibilities, but it goes a long way towards showing that you care. When you do something extra like acknowledging an employee's special day, you go beyond the conventional relationship and earn trust in the process.

Communicate ... Communicate ... Communicate

Improving your communication is another important way to gain trust. The more openly and honestly you communicate, the more trust you will have in your relationships. The frequency of your communication with your supervisor and your employees should not be underestimated. Direct, honest, timely, and caring communication builds trust.

Keep Your Employees Informed

We all want to be "in the know." Take the time to keep your employees informed about what is happening within the organization. The more people feel informed about their organization, the better they feel about their participation in that organization. When you do not have the answer or are unsure of the reason for a particular decision, be honest with your employees and do whatever you can to get more information to them as soon as possible.

> *Direct, honest, timely, and caring communication builds trust.*

Use a *Real* Open Door Policy

Most managers say they have an open door policy. However, employees are quick to discover that, although the door may be open, the mind is closed. If you have an open door policy, it means you welcome people to come to your office with their ideas, comments, complaints, and suggestions. It also means you are open to actively listen and honestly respond to those who come to see you.

Encourage Others to Express Contrary Viewpoints

Let people know you expect them to challenge and disagree with you. When they do, let them state their case. Do not interrupt. Look for areas of agreement and be willing to see the other's perspective. Once you have a clear understanding of their view, clarify the points that you support and those you cannot support. Provide a thorough explanation as to why you disagree. Help other people understand your perspective by speaking clearly and providing examples and illustrations to clarify your points.

Do Not Shoot the Messenger

Nothing destroys trust and credibility more than shooting the messenger. Unfortunately, this is a common problem in many organizations. A good leader understands that, in today's complex organizations, people are required to relay information. If you shoot the messenger one too many times, not only will the messenger not come back again, but everyone else will do whatever it takes to keep negative information from you.

Encourage Employees to Share Information

If your employees rely solely on you to keep them informed, you will quickly become overwhelmed, and the employees will not have all the information they need to do a quality job. Let your staff know you expect them to share information on a regular basis. Actively involve others in giving updates and sharing other relevant information.

Promptly Respond to Communication from Others

A general rule of thumb is to respond to people within 24 hours at the most. A better rule of thumb for some people would be to respond within four hours. Different people have different response expectations. When someone sends you an email, letter, or phone message, respond to that person as promptly as possible to inform them what actions you are taking in response to their email or request for information. Even if you cannot respond with a complete answer or solution right away, let them know you are working on it and will get back to them ASAP. Then, follow through on your promise.

Keep Your Manager Informed

Managers differ in the amount of information they wish to receive from the people they manage. Take the time to discover what your boss expects from you. How often does he or she expect to hear from you? Does he or she prefer written information (reports or status updates) or a weekly face-to-face meeting? What types of decisions does he or she expect to be consulted on? When can you make decisions on your own? How much detail does he or she like? If you cannot readily find the answers to these questions, set up a meeting with your boss to address these questions. Remember, no one likes surprises, and that includes your boss.

Practice the Concept of "No Surprises"

A wife once said to her husband, "If you're going to surprise me, put it in a small jewelry box." As this remark implies, most surprises you receive are negative.

Examples at work might include

- An employee does not solve a customer's problem, resulting in a complaint that filters up to your level;
- Senior management changes a policy or procedure but does not inform your department of the changes;
- You believed you were receiving a promotion, only to find out someone else received the offer.

The more you eliminate negative surprises from relationships with your supervisor and your employees, the stronger the bonds of trust. One of the best ways to eliminate negative surprises is through clear and frequent communication.

Set Clear Expectations

Clear expectations are critical to building trust. The clearer you are about what you expect from others and what others can expect from you, the easier it is to build trust.

Be Honest

Everyone agrees that honesty builds trust. What we want to

emphasize is the power of honesty, especially when it costs you something to be truthful. For example, if you were to go to your employees and tell them there was going to be a layoff in two months, the chances are your employees will be unhappy with you and your news. But, they will remember that you gave them all the information you had as soon as you had it. Or, suppose you witness someone unknowingly drop a $100 bill. You call attention to the lost bill and return it to the person. It "cost" you $100, but this person now perceives you as honest and is more inclined to trust you. We gain the most trust through honesty when that honesty actually costs us something.

Care about Your Supervisor's and Your Employees' Personal and Professional Success

Do you know what is important to your employees? Can you name their spouses and children? When your people need help, do they find you approachable and understanding? Do you support your boss when they have an issue?

When your actions demonstrate to your supervisor and your employees that you genuinely care about their personal and professional success, they will find it easier to trust you and the decisions you make in your leadership role.

Have Their Backs

Trust in the workplace happens when everyone feels they are free to try new ideas, encouraged to accept new and challenging projects, and, at the professional development level, are working to push themselves forward. This also means mistakes will happen. Great leaders encourage and support people to try new ideas, even when they know mistakes will result. Innovation is what drives the entire organization forward, but innovation cannot happen if people are not given the opportunity to try new things.

Employees know they are not always going to be perfect. As a leader, you want employees to have the freedom to make mistakes and learn from them. You want people who are willing to take risks in the hopes of creating new products, services, and ideas that will ultimately improve the condition of your team or organization. It is preferable to have people try and fail than to not try at all. People can learn from failure if they use the experience to grow and gain valuable perspectives to apply to their next project. A good leader will help this process.

When people are consistently sharing ideas, project updates, successes, and failures, they learn to accept feedback, continue learning, and take action. Are you creating an environment where people are encouraged to take risks and make mistakes? Doing so demonstrates and nurtures mutual trust.

Under-Promise and Over-Deliver

We spoke with an employee who was smart and motivated, and cheerfully gave 110 percent all the time, every day, including weekends, nights, and holidays. This employee never expected any special treatment, and was the consummate team player. His boss told him he would receive a bonus for all the extra work. But the bonus was not approved. The corporate policy of providing "time off" was used instead, so the employee was told to take time off as compensation. But the work and the requirements still existed. Not only was the employee unable to take off time, he had been promised money that never arrived. He felt the organization deceived him and he quit four months later.

Do not make promises if you cannot deliver. Instead, under-promise and over-deliver.

Shoot Straight with New Hires

Organizations need to be very careful about what they promise people during the hiring process. Many organizations and excited human resources managers try to paint the rosiest picture possible of the opportunities available at the company. When the employee arrives, they are quickly disillusioned and feel subjected to a bait-and-switch. When hiring new people, be truthful. Tell them the good, the bad, and the ugly. Tell them what challenges they might face, and make sure they make a well-informed decision to come to work for your organization.

Shoot straight. The reputation of your organization will attract new employees. The reality of your organization's culture is what will retain new employees. Don't exaggerate benefits or dangle possible benefits that are years in the future. When the employee shows up and finds the promised benefit, project, or promotion is several years in the future, they feel betrayed; trust is destroyed.

Get to Know Your People

We witnessed an amazing example of what great leaders do to build trust within their workforce. A new boss was joining the organization. She sent out emails letting people know she was coming, and she set up an anonymous way for employees to let her know if they felt there were important things for this new leader to know. This new leader made it clear that team members could speak to her about anything, whether it was related to personnel, work environment, office support, or career development. She wanted to know what was on people's minds and what she needed to address to build an even stronger team and more supportive work environment. She assured everyone that all comments would remain confidential and anonymous. She wanted honest feedback.

When she arrived, she asked everyone to meet with her for an orientation and asked everyone for their written goals for the year before the meeting. The more senior people thought this was a wasted exercise and complained.

When she met with everyone individually for "orientation," she did not review the goals. She informed the employees that she had used the goals to get to know people before their meeting. During the orientation, she said, "I want you to orient me. Tell me how you got here, how you came to work here, and something interesting that's going on in your life."

Everyone had expected a baseline performance evaluation. It was not a performance evaluation, and the leader did not talk about herself. The entire meeting was all about the employee. She listened the entire time, speaking only to follow up with interested questions about the employees. Every single employee walked out of their meeting feeling valued, appreciated, and listened to. It was one of the most effective techniques we have ever seen a new leader utilize. When employees feel cared for, trust for their leader comes much more easily.

Make Their Priorities YOUR Priorities

We watched an accounting firm with very talented and highly motivated people suddenly experience a decrease in morale. Some of the accountants were working on some very specialized clients' issues, which required certain processes and certain forms. The problem was, the administrative assistant who had electronic access to these forms had left, and no one knew how or where to get them.

Repeated requests to the manager went largely ignored because it simply was not the manager's priority. He had no idea how the forms were used or why they were important. The team of talented accountants was stuck. Weeks went by and the employees became frustrated and angry because they felt the boss was ignoring them and did not care about this project. One senior accountant complained to us, "I can't move forward because I don't have what I need to do my job. If my boss and this firm cared about me, they would make sure I had what I needed to do this job."

> *When employees feel cared for, trust for their leader comes much more easily.*

Your employees' priorities must be your priorities.

If you want your people to trust you, they have to believe what they feel is important is equally important to you.

Structure Work for Individual and Team Success

Leaders need to know their people and know what tools they need in order to be successful at work. Sometimes this means more telework, flexible hours, alternative work sites, and using technology to connect instead of a time clock.

This does not mean coddling employees or making exceptions repeatedly for people who are not performing. This means understanding what is important to them, knowing what motivates them, and treating people as individuals instead of as commodities. To build mutual trust, focus on holding people accountable for results rather than face time or hours worked.

Give People Honest, Direct, Helpful, and Immediate Feedback

One of our military examples comes from an Army general, whose temper was legendary and explosive. He was impatient, demanding, and he "did not suffer fools well," as everyone knew. If you were wrong, he let you know immediately and, sometimes, in front of everyone else. Loudly! He wanted information and it had to be accurate.

He sounds like an ogre, and, yet, his officers and troops loved him. Why?

"We always know exactly where we are with him," explained one mid-level officer. "If you're wrong, he lets you know right away. If he is mad, you know it!"

"And so does everyone else!" chimed in another officer.

When we asked if they trusted him, every single person responded with an enthusiastic yes. "Absolutely. He is totally straight with everyone. He doesn't care if you are another general or a colonel or a major. He is a no-BS guy with everyone."

Another officer added, "Plus, once he explodes, it's over. He expects you to fix the problem and not let it happen again. You screwed up and you know it, but he still lets you know that he trusts you to do your job and take care of your people."

Great leaders know that being honest with employees, especially when things are tough, builds trust. Great leaders trust their people and give them the opportunities to live up to expectations.

Don't Waste Your One Chance

You only get one chance, and that applies to businesses, too. Whether it is a fast food restaurant or your local barber, the first experience with their product or service generally determines your lifelong impression of that company. Some employees will only give you one chance before deciding whether or not they trust you.

> *Great leaders trust their people and give them the opportunities to live up to expectations.*

Building trust takes time. If you do what you say you're going to do, do more than is expected, openly communicate often, practice the concept of "no surprises," practice honesty even when it costs you something, and really care about an individual's personal and professional success, you will find it easier to build relationships based on trust.

> *It can take weeks, months, and even years to build trust, but mere minutes to destroy it.*

Gaining and retaining the trust of a team is one of the most difficult things a leader can do. It can take weeks, months, and even years to build trust, but mere minutes to destroy it.

7 Tips for Building Trust

1. Give employees as much information as you can, both good and bad.
2. Respecting others means respecting their time.
3. Know that information travels fast so get ahead of the problem.
4. Spend time with your people and listen to what is important to them.
5. Make your people's priorities YOUR priorities.
6. Under-promise and over-deliver to your employees.
7. Structure your team's work to best enable their success.

3

They Just Don't Care!

I worry that business leaders are more interested
in material gain than they are in having the patience
to build up a strong organization, and a strong
organization starts with caring for their people.

—John Wooden

We met with a senior vice president who barely inter-
acted with his employees or peers. When he was around his
employees, he did not greet or acknowledge them, ask how
they were doing at work, or inquire about their families. He
gave the impression he was always too busy doing other,
far more important things and did not have the time to be
considerate or even polite. He was rude and abrupt.

Almost all his communication was done through email, but
he was not good with email either. He did not respond to
emails in a timely manner. His team grew increasingly frustrated and developed "workarounds." After sending a third
email request for information necessary to help advance
their projects, team members would trudge down to his
office and ask for the answer directly. His biggest problem,

to no one's surprise, was that he did not communicate with his team unless he deemed it absolutely essential.

When we asked him why he did not attempt to communicate or build relationships with his team members and peers, he honestly responded, "I really don't care about them. We're paid to do our jobs. My priority is to get my job done, not to make team members feel good or act like I really care." Ouch!

This leader had several challenges. First, he did not see a reason or need to interact or care. Second, in the beginning of the coaching process, he decided that if caring was really that important in his leadership position, he could fake it. He tried that, but he was terrible at faking that he cared. As you can imagine, relationships between this leader and his direct reports were damaged even further by his insincere efforts. His people saw right through him. Productivity and morale declined. His top talent left for other opportunities, and, presumably, better leadership.

As we have discussed, leaders may or may not have a title. What true leaders always have are relationships with people who are motivated to follow them. In our example, this vice president had a title and a position on the organizational chart, but he lacked genuine relationships with his team members and was certainly not a leader.

Path to Failure

Leaders who are perceived as uncaring towards their people or organization exhibit several specific, and habitual, behaviors that have earned them that reputation. Every manager may at one time or another slip up, but it is the consistent display of these behaviors that result in a leader earning a reputation for not caring. Based on our research, the following are the most common behaviors that communicate to employees a lack of concern or care.

Not Listening

One of the fastest ways to let someone know you do not care about them or value their opinion is to not listen.

We have seen leaders cut off their counterparts while they were still talking, walk away from an employee while they were trying to answer his question, and/or answer a call while someone else was still speaking. We witnessed another manager tell her team that meetings were called to make sure people were still at work at 4 p.m., not for discussion or for people to provide feedback or exchange ideas.

An equally effective way to demonstrate you are not listening is to not take action or follow up on what you've been told. Far too many leaders believe they are great multi-taskers and perfectly capable of responding to an email or answering the phone while someone else is attempting to communicate with them. Failing to give the other person your undivided attention unequivocally communicates just how little you care about them and what they have to say.

Not Spending Time with Team Members

Failing to dedicate time to the growth and development of their direct reports is one surefire way for managers to communicate how little they care about their team members. These managers are more concerned with getting their own work done instead of taking the time to check in with their team members. When team members ask for some of their manager's time, these managers will try to manage the relationship or solve the problem by email or any other way that takes the least amount of time or effort. To an uncaring manager, meeting face-to-face instead of resolving the problem by email or phone is a waste of their valuable time.

As a result, employees do not feel their roles and careers will progress in this environment. Sadly, they are correct.

Managing the Status Quo

A lot of managers embrace the philosophy that if employees have a problem, they will inform their manager. These managers are not proactive about learning what their employees are working on or to see if they need any support from their leader. If employees are not telling them there's a problem, then these managers assume everything is fine. But, if a manager hasn't developed a relationship of trust, the employee will never inform them of a problem until it's too late to fix or the employee quits out of frustration.

Not Working for the Team

Uncaring managers are, first and foremost, concerned about their own needs and goals. That means others below them on the organizational chart are there to serve their manager first and get their own jobs accomplished second. Uncaring managers have no problem giving employees last minute rush projects to do, even when the manager has been aware of the project and the deadline for days or weeks. Uncaring managers ask employees to work nights and weekends to help meet organizational goals when the manager failed to plan the project. These managers also find it difficult to grant an employee's request for time off if it will create any additional work for the manager.

What many managers don't understand is they work for their team. A leader's job is to support the team and make sure they have what they need to get the job done. True leaders know organizations flourish when a leader practices servant leadership. The diagram below demonstrates the hierarchy of servant leadership.

*The boss has to know that taking care of customers
starts with taking care of employees.*

Pretending to Care

The boss has to know that taking care of customers starts with taking care of employees. The only thing worse than leaders who communicate they do not care are managers who say they care but whose actions clearly demonstrate the opposite. We coached one manager who repeatedly told his team he was fighting hard with senior management to give the team raises and a flexible schedule. Truth be told, this manager had little credibility with senior management and never made either request on behalf of his team. When the team discovered the manager was not telling the truth, they felt betrayed and lost respect for him as a leader.

Withholding Information

We work with managers who take pride in communicating information to their team solely on a "need-to-know" basis. These managers either believe they are too busy to keep their employees in the loop, or they play the "I've got a secret" game where they intentionally withhold information from others to make themselves feel more important by being "in the know." This secretive manifestation of insecurity by the leader results in employees who are hesitant to make decisions, spend considerable time reworking projects based on information that arrives late, and find out later that multiple people are working on the same projects. Not communicating with employees in a complete and timely manner tells them the manager feels they are not important enough to receive the information and does not care about them or their success.

Acting like a Bully

One leader we worked with had a hot and short temper. He yelled at and spoke in a condescending manner to his direct reports and peers. When we asked him why he treated people this way, he responded, "I am an honest communicator and people deserve to know the truth." We fully support communicating the truth, but the truth can be communicated without acting like a schoolyard bully. When we asked him if his goal in communicating the truth was to help or to hurt his team members, he replied, "I really don't care if I hurt their feelings. It's more important for them to know the truth." His idea of truth was his perception. Those around him thought he was profoundly insecure and just plain mean. His "truth" was not perceived as such by anyone else.

Not Providing Growth and Development Opportunities for Others

Uncaring managers do not take the time to coach and develop their employees, nor do they provide ongoing growth opportunities.

Studies show that between 33 and 44 percent of a company's turnover is related to a lack of development and growth opportunities for employees. In our own research conducting over 400 Leadership Development Assessments (360), the Best of the Best leaders are rated 9 percent higher when it comes to investing their time and energy into developing their people. Providing employees with growth and development opportunities tells employees you believe and trust they are capable of doing even more and you care about their future.

Offering Weak or No Performance Reviews

The performance appraisal should articulate where an employee's strengths are, as well as identify areas for growth and development. Employees can tell during the review how much effort a manager puts into accurately evaluating their performance. An employee shared details about the performance review given to her by her manager. She said, "A ten-year-old child could have completed this review in less than five minutes. It had a check mark in a box to identify the rating and next to each rating, were three or four words like, 'doing a good job' or 'meets team expectations.'" This employee summed up her boss well when she said, "He doesn't care about me. If he doesn't care about me, why should I go out of my way to care about him or this department?"

We worked with another manager who took pride in telling everyone that "no one can get the company's highest rating, no matter how good their performance." This declaration only broadcasted that the manager did not have an objective and standard way to measure performance. If they did, in fact, have an objective and standardized way to measure performance, it was an unfair performance management system.

Employees deserve more than 10 or 15 minutes of time once a year. Performance appraisals should be a formalized meeting of what the employee already knows about their performance, their workplace contribution, and the path to advance in the company or industry.

Rejecting or Not Acting on Feedback

One of the best ways to demoralize employees is to ask for feedback and then act on none of it. When leaders reject or fail to act on feedback, team members usually stop providing feedback to their manager.

One organization we worked with prided themselves on collecting feedback to help their leaders learn and grow. We discovered, however, the company had assessment exhaustion. The CEO loved assessments and found a new one for the organization to conduct every six months or so. The problem was they never acted on any of the feedback to improve the organization. Before we agree to conduct Employee Engagement Surveys or Leadership Development Assessments (360) for our clients, we confirm the leader's commitment to take action. Actions trump intentions. Knowledge is helpful, but leaders need to act.

Swearing at Work

Some managers do not realize how demoralizing profane language can be for some members of the team. If foul language comes out of your mouth in an angry tone, you can create a situation where some team members feel disgusted, tense, or uncomfortable. Many managers do not know what type of language crosses the line for individual members of their team. Most likely, each team member will have a different boundary and comfort zone when it comes to swearing at work. If the manager swears and others view it as acceptable, they will likely swear as well. Managers who care about their team members choose their words wisely and will not risk using language that makes others feel uncomfortable and/or offended.

One of our leaders handled the language issue really well. The first time someone used an inappropriate word, she asked in a friendly manner, "Is that really the most descriptive word you can find for this situation?" The manager then responded with a series of other non-offensive adjectives.

Great Military Example of Caring

We asked people in one of our leadership training sessions, "What type of characteristics would you use to describe the Captain and Commanding Officer of a U.S. Navy aircraft carrier?" The people we interviewed gave the following answers:

- A directive leadership style.
- A great track record of naval and leadership success.
- A fighter pilot.
- A clear communicator of what they want done.
- The ability to command respect.

Captains of aircraft carriers are responsible for 5,600 young men and women who live and work together for several months at a time while at sea. Surprisingly, not one person interviewed listed *caring* as an essential leadership attribute of a CO. In our military experience, we encountered fabulous examples of extraordinary leadership. When commanding a city at sea during wartime, a good CO must care about his or her people. It is extremely difficult to balance work, training, and boredom with life or death emergency situations. We want to profile how one CO conveyed his sense of responsibility for taking care of his people.

The following email was sent out by Captain Karl Thomas, Commanding Officer of the U.S. aircraft carrier USS Carl

Vinson, to his entire crew during a forward-deployed operation. They had been at sea for seven months. Imagine how
hard it is to be at sea, working nonstop, for even a few weeks.
Now, add in the stress of combat operations, separation from
family, and missing holidays, anniversaries, and the birth of
your child. It is a stressful situation.

Shipmates,

We're in the home stretch of a long period at sea. Not
just a long period between port calls, but just plain
long when you think of how much time we've been
away from home. I have the good fortune of looking
across the entire team and seeing/hearing/watching
the overall "tone" of the ship. The vast majority of you
are doing exceptionally well and the team continues to
perform and work well together. We are maintaining
our stride. However, there are a few of our shipmates
that are struggling, and time and again you--the
concerned shipmate--are the one that is identifying
these individuals and encouraging them to seek assis-
tance. Thank you for having the courage to intervene!

We have just under 30 days left in the Arabian Gulf
flying missions in support of Operation Inherent
Resolve. Just under 30 days to persevere and continue
to follow procedures, to not cut corners, to get enough
rest so that we can tackle each day fresh... and 30 days
to be kind, tolerant, and supportive of one another.

Perseverance and tolerance. Those are two traits that
every one of us needs to embrace. Everyone has their
bad days. Not everyone agrees on the solution to an
issue. Not everyone is in their happy spot. This is the
time in deployment where it is critical that we look for
ways to prop one another up. Now is when the kind
word instead of the cold-hearted barb is the better

choice. Now is when positive-toned leadership is more effective than negative-toned leadership. Now is the time to smile and say good morning or to shake a hand. Positive attitude goes a long way toward influencing others. Being attentive to other people's concerns and knowing when your shipmate needs encouragement is the sign of a great shipmate.

Quite frankly, I'm counting on each and every one of you to look out for each other. XO and I say it on the 1MC every day to "take care of your shipmates" and we mean it. A concerned shipmate is our best defense for a Sailor that is having a hard time.

Thanks for all you do every day and for the sacrifices you are making on this extremely long deployment. The light is truly burning brighter, and we want to finish strong with the entire team intact. Be tolerant of one another. Persevere to the finish line!

All the best!
CAPT "T"

Captain Karl Thomas
Commanding Officer
USS CARL VINSON (CVN 70)

There is one sentence about the mission of the crew, but every other word of the email conveys that Captain Thomas really cares about every one of his shipmates and is asking the rest of the crew to do the same. It is a reminder to watch out for each other. Is this the type of leadership we want to follow into combat? Yes.

Most of us do not ask people to sleep at work for months at a time, and we do not experience the risk involved with being in a wartime scenario, but the leadership principles are the same.

> *In leadership, caring is not a sign of weakness.*

The impact of this communication on the art of leadership is huge. People find it easy to support and follow leaders who really care. In leadership, caring is not a sign of weakness. As this email demonstrates, caring and watching out for others is a sign of great strength.

Prescription for Caring Success

Why don't leaders take more action to demonstrate they care about their people? Many reply they are too busy. While there are limited time and resources, there is always time to genuinely care for the people who devote the majority of their waking time to your organization. We contend that no one is ever too busy to take care of his or her people. If you care, you make the time.

The following are the practices leaders put into action to demonstrate they genuinely care about their team members and value their contributions:

Celebrate When Things Go Right

Leaders who care take the time to celebrate the successes of their team. They take the time to acknowledge success and make people feel valued by calling positive attention to their accomplishments.

Honor Others During Difficult Times

In the military, tragedy happens. Great leaders take the time to honor the wounded and fallen for doing what is right. Leaders show up when times are the toughest. In business, although the examples are fewer, there are times when tragedy strikes. When a team member passes away or an employee experiences tragedy in their family, this is the time for a leader to step up and center the team's focus on honoring the employee or their family.

Encourage Work/Life Balance

Leaders who care exemplify work/life balance. They also encourage their employees to be accountable for living a schedule that promotes a positive balance between work and home life.

In good times, anyone can lead. It is when things go wrong that people need true, strong, honest, and caring leadership.

Thanks to technology, the line between personal and professional time is blurred. It is more and more difficult to get time where we are totally away from work.

One leader told us she liked to answer emails late at night after her kids went to bed. The problem with sending emails late at night, she told us, is that her direct reports felt compelled to respond back to her emails immediately, regardless of the late hour. This manager really cared about her employees having down time at home, and, even though she told them NOT to respond to her late night emails, they did anyway. She made the decision to schedule the emails she completed at night for delivery during working hours the next day.

Show Up

Mary's first meeting with one of her Navy bosses, the commanding officer of the base, went pretty much as expected until he said, "Oh, and if any of your people or their family members go to the hospital and are admitted, you need to let my office know."

I was a little confused. This guy was really busy. His assistant was constantly trying to keep him on schedule. He arrived at the office at 6 a.m. and often stayed way past 6 p.m.

I wanted to make sure I understood. I thought he was micro-managing me so I asked for clarification. "You have a lot to worry about. Why do you want to know whether or not my people get sick?"

He matter-of-factly replied, "Because they are my people, too. And, if they are in the hospital, for any reason at all, I show up."

I persisted. Was there a threshold involved? Did the people actually have to be seriously ill? What if they just broke an arm or a pinky finger? What if they were having their tonsils out? What if they were in the hospital for just a few hours?

He reiterated, "I show up. And you do, too. That is what we do."

Got it, boss.

Sure enough, a few months later, one of my people landed in the hospital. I dutifully left the relevant information with my boss's office and then I drove the 20 miles to the hospital, parked my car, and trekked to my sailor's hospital room. About 20 minutes after I arrived, so did the commanding officer.

Three things happened:

First, my sailor's eyes lit up when the *big* boss called my sailor by his name and asked how he was doing. My sailor sat up straighter in the hospital bed. He smiled.

The visit was a huge morale booster for the patient. He visibly perked up. He felt cared for because this important leader took the time to check on him. My sailor felt like he was more than a number, more than a name on a list of employees. The commanding officer showed that he cared at a time when the young man needed to know that he had support that extended throughout the entire organization.

Second, the arrival of a Navy Captain (that is one rank below an admiral or general) in a military hospital generated some attention. While the staff had ignored me (I was a mere Lieutenant Commander at the time), suddenly hospital personnel gave my sailor a little more attention. Having a Navy Captain show up to visit made staff take notice of his case.

Third, my boss reiterated that it is when things go wrong or when times are tough that our people need us to show up the most. He asked me to keep him informed and told me to let him know if he could help. And he meant it.

It is easy to show up when things are going well. Most of us have stories about fair-weather friends and co-workers who abandon us when we are going through a difficult time or are experiencing a life crisis. This commanding officer made it clear that leadership is most important when it isn't glamorous. Leadership means sacrificing our own time, energy, and resources.

> *Leadership is most important when supporting people isn't glamorous, easy, or convenient.*

Want to be a great leader? Show up, show you care, and show you can help.

Encourage People to Talk, Socialize, and Connect

Martin Seligman, one of the preeminent thought leaders on self-esteem, states that connecting with others in a meaningful way leads to better mental and physical health, as well as speedier recovery from illness. Providing your employees with encouragement is great. But, even better than providing canned encouragement is taking the time to genuinely talk, socialize, and connect with others on your team. A few minutes spent with one of your team members today can be a valuable investment for years to come.

Leaders sometimes fail to recognize how important socializing is for their employees. Yes, they do talk about some personal issues, but most often, when left alone, employees discuss work issues, work problems, and ways to solve those problems. Informal socialization helps people be better, more productive workers.

One of our coaching executives was proud of himself for getting rid of the employee break room where employees gathered for lunch. Two things happened. First, because there was no longer a place at work for them to eat, they left the building for lunch. They were away from work longer.

Second, they stopped having lunch with each other. They ran errands and went to their children's schools. As a result, productivity declined because the CEO thought he was saving time and space.

Step in at the Right Time

We always find it easier to be compassionate when we think: "How would I feel if I were in their shoes?" "What would help me if I were in that situation?" There's an emotional video on YouTube of an NBA basketball game with the Portland Trail Blazers where the little girl singing the national anthem forgets the words. The fans, the players, the referees, and even her parents stand there in stunned disbelief, unsure of what to do. Then Maurice Cheeks, head coach of the Trail Blazers, walks out to center court and joins this little girl in singing the national anthem. She sings along with the coach, and the crowd is clearly relieved and happy. That is both compassion and leadership displayed at the right time.

Listen

Strong personalities often want to solve problems, and they have a strong urge to tell their subordinates and counterparts what to do. Compassion is about listening and trying to understand what the other person is thinking and feeling. Nelson Mandela learned the importance of listening from watching his father, Chief Jongintaba, interact with his tribe during meetings of the court. When Mandela conducted meetings, he listened first and spoke last. When leaders listen, they respond compassionately, whether by offering advice, providing solutions, allowing people to make mistakes, being empathetic, or saying nothing.

Take Action

Listening is great. But when you listen and, then, fail to take action, people are inclined to think you didn't really hear what was being said. When a team member or customer lets you know they need your support, failing to take action undermines your credibility and your character. When you agree to support a colleague, add it to your list, and only cross it off when the commitment has been completed.

The road to hell is paved with good intentions. If you intend to do something, do it.

Give Your Time

The greatest gift you can give someone is your time. Giving your time demonstrates that someone is really important to you. As leaders, we have myriad goals we want to accomplish. In the end, it is the relationships you create, build, and nourish that truly matter. Someone once told us, "It's better to give someone your time because, no matter what you accomplish or acquire, you won't be taking it with you

when you die. They don't put trailer hitches on hearses."
So true.

That doesn't mean you need to spend all your time doting on
employees, but it does mean managing your schedule so you
can celebrate with teams when they do well, advise teams
when they need guidance, and support teams when they run
into roadblocks.

Show Gratitude

Your *attitude* is extremely important in becoming a servant
leader. Do you consider the opportunity to lead your team
a privilege? Are you grateful for each and every one of your
colleagues and the daily contributions they make that lead
to your success and the success of the organization? Most
importantly, do your team members, colleagues and internal
and external customers know you are grateful for the opportunity to serve them and to help them achieve their goals?

Have a more grateful attitude and remind yourself that you
wanted this job. You wanted to make a difference, and every
day is a privilege. When serving in the Navy, people would
occasionally thank us for our service. It's gratifying that
civilians appreciate service men and women, but it is also
somewhat of a shock every time someone says it because
we signed up to serve. We never expected to be thanked for
the privilege of leading young men and women. Each and
every day, even during the bad days, we felt it was a privilege
to serve. Other people turn over their sons and daughters
to us and expect us to train them, lead them, watch over
them, and help them grow into their next careers. It is a huge
responsibility and an honor.

Is being a great leader difficult? Yes. It takes time and effort
and a different skill set. If it were easy, every great manager

would also be a great leader. Is being a caring leader even harder? Yes, but by focusing on your people and putting these caring attributes into action daily, you will see the rewards—in organizational results, emotional engagement and commitment of your team, and the true joy of being a leader who genuinely cares.

7 Tips for Showing You Truly Care

1. Recognize that your direct reports are people with thoughts, feelings, and unique backgrounds.
2. Demonstrate empathy.
3. Communicate by listening attentively, responding respectfully, and taking appropriate action.
4. Connect with your employees and get to know them by talking and socializing.
5. Encourage and respect a healthy work/life balance.
6. Take a genuine interest in your employees' developmental goals and commit to helping them achieve their aspirations.
7. Adopt an attitude of gratitude toward employees and peers, and recognize that leading them is a privilege.

4

They are Unfair

Win or lose, do it fairly.

—Knute Rockne

In one of our client Fortune 500 companies, an executive (we'll call her Jamie) has seven people who report directly to her. One of her direct reports (we'll call her Sarah) was under-performing. Jamie discussed putting Sarah on a corrective action/performance improvement plan because Sarah was not making her goals. Worse, Sarah did not seem motivated to improve. Sarah refused to follow Jamie's advice on taking the steps needed to help her achieve her goals.

Jamie decided to formalize Sarah's failures in a write-up. Sarah was not written up for missing her goals but for refusing to follow Jamie's advice and implementing a set of recommended actions. Jamie felt Sarah was ignoring her guidance and, thus, was violating a direct order—an affront to Jamie as a leader.

In coaching Jamie, we asked, "Were there any other managers on the team who were not hitting their goals?"

Jamie admitted four of her seven direct reports had not made their quotas, and two others refused to implement her directions. Sarah, however, was the only one who received a formal written warning.

Sure enough, when the performance feedback was delivered to Sarah, Sarah felt singled out and took a walk down the hall to human resources. Sarah complained that Jamie's treatment was unfair because the other team members with similar results were not held accountable for their poor performance. Unfortunately for Jamie, in this case, Sarah was right. Singling out one employee when others on the team were exhibiting the same behaviors and generating the same poor results was unfair.

People will forgive a certain amount of rudeness, tardiness, or other disruptive behaviors exhibited by their boss, but being perceived as an unfair leader is a difficult reputation for a boss to overcome. Many people are highly affected by injustice. They will forgive sheer stupidity, but they seldom forget or forgive perceived unfairness.

Leaders should strive for fairness; however, it is important to note that not all unfairness exhibited by leaders produces a bad team outcome.

In research published in the *Journal of Applied Psychology*, Adam Stoverink and his colleagues examined how bosses treat the members of their teams and how that influences team dynamics. The researchers split participants into small teams and gave some of the teams a fair, polite supervisor and others an unfair, disrespectful supervisor. The teams with the unfair boss reported less satisfaction with and trust in their supervisor than the teams that were treated fairly.

Surprisingly, these unfairly treated teams also reported higher levels of team cohesiveness measured by their responses to questions like "My team stuck together," "My team helped each other out," and "My team members got along with each other." Is this rude and unfair leadership strategy worth implementing to create a united team that produces positive results? Hardly, unless you are a Steve Jobs-type of leader with world-changing results to back you up. There is nothing more powerful than a team united behind one goal: to get their leader fired.

Steve Jobs was notorious for being moody, rude, tyrannical, egotistical, spiteful, controlling, and uncompromising. Walter Isaacson's best-selling biography of Jobs offers a revealing look at what the author calls *Good Steve* and *Bad Steve*. Good Steve was brilliant, charming, and charismatic. As a result of Good Steve's leadership, Apple is recognized as one of the all-time greatest companies that have changed the world. Steve Jobs had futuristic sense about what customers wanted and was committed to turning existing technology into something completely new. With a commitment to quality and design that was second to none, he turned ordinary Apple customers into raving fans for life. But, Bad Steve was not exempt from the downside of being a difficult leader to work with and one that some would consider unfair. In 1985, Apple's new CEO fired Steve Jobs from his own company.

Employers who violate rules of fairness may or may not be punished by the law. But, they are punished by reduced employee engagement, productivity, and loyalty.

Path to Failure

What causes people to perceive the actions of their leaders as unfair? What makes employees bristle and push back? Chances are you have heard someone on your team say, "That's not fair." That accusation likely stung because you strive to be ethical, honest, and, above all, a fair leader.

The term "fair" means different things to different people, which is part of the problem. Leaders are usually accused of being unfair when others believe they have not treated everyone equally or in a manner consistent with the company's rules, policies, and past practices.

The following are some of the most common examples employees tell us, with conviction, make an unfair boss.

Playing Favorites

The Merriam-Webster dictionary defines favoritism as, "The unfair practice of treating some people better than others." This next example seems petty, but actually cost one manager her job. This manager was responsible for multiple branches of a financial institution. The manager let everyone know she was committed to responding to vacation requests from her direct reports within 48 hours. She also let the managers know she would honor vacation requests on a first-come, first-request-granted basis. Sounds like a great policy to ensure fairness.

The policy worked well until the manager she liked the least requested a week off over the Thanksgiving break to spend time with her family in the Bahamas. Instead of approving this manager's vacation request, the boss sent out an email to her other direct reports asking if any of them were planning to take the same week off. Some observers may view her as a proactive manager who realized that many people may be planning to take Thanksgiving week off.

Maybe so, but here is why the problem got ugly. The manager violated her own policy with regards to the beach-bound hopeful. She did not respond to the request for vacation approval. The direct report sent an email three times asking if her vacation was approved. Each time, the email was ignored. Two weeks before the employee was to leave on her trip, her request for vacation was denied because other managers had requested the same week off and their requests were quickly approved. The subordinate (who had already purchased plane tickets and booked a condo) went to human resources and provided the facts necessary to override the manager's denial and gain approval for her vacation. Consistent with company policy, human resources had to approve the employee's vacation. This manager could have built a reputation for fairness if she had followed through on her commitment to process requests fairly and abide by her stated policies regarding vacation requests. Instead, the situation snowballed into an inquiry that uncovered multiple similar occurrences and favoritism. The result of that inquiry led to the termination of the senior manager.

Telling Someone *Exactly* How to Do their Job, and Being Wrong

This is a complicated scenario. There are times when leaders hire a new employee or need a very specific outcome, and there is a need for the employee to know exactly what they need to do and how they should do it. Most often, this situation does not fit into the category of unfairness. It *does*, however, become a problem when the boss lacks technical, industry, or detail competence, and still tries to tell the employee how to do their job. This is unfair to the employee because it sets them up for failure. If the employee accomplishes the job but they did not do so using the methods dictated, they can be faulted by the boss. If they follow the boss's process and the result is failure, then the employee did not do the job they were hired to do. This is unfair, and it is arrogant to think you can tell someone how to do something that you know nothing about.

We were taught that when it comes to giving technically competent people feedback about how to do their job, "you can tell someone what to do, or you can tell them how to do it. You cannot do both."

As soon as you delegate the responsibility and clearly communicate the goal and the desired outcome, you lose the right to tell the team member exactly how to do the job. In this rapidly changing world, a leader should allow flexibility on how their people can get a job accomplished.

Kissing Up and Kicking Down

Unfair bosses masterfully maintain their personal reputations with their bosses and other executives higher up in the organization. Going up the ladder, these unfair bosses are responsive, supportive, and respectful. They carefully manage the information conveyed to those above them to ensure they look great. These are also the bosses who create a watertight door to guard against any of their direct reports having either access to, or open communication with, those above them in the hierarchy. To maintain their positive reputation with their superiors, unfair bosses are notorious for not providing their peers and direct reports with the same level of responsiveness, support, and respect they provide to senior leaders in the organization.

We met one vice president of human resources who was in charge of scheduling monthly leadership meetings. In what we determined was a deliberate attempt to make other VPs look bad in front of the CEO, the HR leader often changed the meeting locations or times, or left some executives off the email distribution list. This resulted in other executives often showing up late, or not at all. Not cool.

Taking Credit

Unfair bosses are masters at utilizing the words "I," "me," or "my" when things go right. Some of these bosses use the self-describing words so often they sound like they are warming up for the opera ... me, me, me; my, my, my; I, I, I. When things go right, unfair bosses are quick to make sure they get credit and ensure that everyone knows what a great job they did. Some of these leaders are bold enough to tell everyone that, without them, the team would fail, thus solidifying their own importance.

Passing Blame

If you work with a boss who unfairly takes all the credit when things go well, you can safely bet they do not take responsibility when things go wrong. Unfair bosses excel at blaming others. The unfairness is amplified when a leader wrongly blames someone else because they did not have their facts straight. The unfair leader then has to either admit they were wrong (which does not happen often) or justify why the team or person still wrongly deserves the blame. Unfair leaders find scapegoats for every possible mistake. Occasionally, we see this extending to personal lives. One employee we interviewed described her boss as the type of person who might as well have a sign on his door that says, "The buck never stops here ... only the kudos." When things go wrong, unfair leaders will find someone else to blame.

Failing to Enforce Accountability

When we coach leaders who are described as unfair because they do not hold team members accountable, the following examples are shared:

- Leader does not have clear goals and expectations for the team member.
- Leader does not like conflict.
- The employee excels at some parts of their job so the boss has made a decision to lower the bar and live with the poor performance in other parts of their job. This is most common when the employee has a particular talent or skill that is hard to find, such as expertise in technology or sales.
- Leader fails to hold certain team members accountable because the team members are well connected to senior leaders in the organization, who support the lack of accountability—nepotism at its finest.
- Leader is too busy doing operational tasks or placating his bosses and chooses not to tackle tough people issues.

Being Moody and/or Rude

In conducting a 360° assessment for a leader, one of her direct reports told us, "When you come back to give her the feedback, I would recommend you come later in the afternoon. Her mood is pretty foul in the mornings."

One of the most difficult reputations for a leader to change is when they are considered moody. Employees should be able to work in a professional and positive environment. When a supervisor flies into fits of rage, sulks, or behaves inconsistently (hissy fits; road rage in the office; refuses to talk to, acknowledge, or work with team members), it is unprofessional. It can easily result in a "creates hostile work environment" allegation.

> *Employees should be able to work in a professional and positive environment.*

When team members work for a moody and rude leader, they will leave if the option is available to them. It is unfair to provide an inconsistent and unpleasant work environment. When unfair managers quit or are eventually fired, they brighten up the whole office on their way out.

Berating Staff in Front of Others

Every good leader knows they should praise in public but provide corrective feedback in private. All too often, we hear stories about managers who explode and censure employees during meetings or within earshot of others. When a boss criticizes one employee in front of others, it accomplishes three things: it makes everyone in the room uncomfortable (thereby causing decreased productivity); it makes people sympathize with the victim; and it makes the boss look like an unfair jerk.

Expressing Demeaning Comments

Unfair leaders have been known to utilize demeaning phrases. Some of these are so outrageous they would be comical if they weren't true.

- You're lucky to have this job.
- You're really lucky to have me as your boss because someone else would have fired you by now.
- I hired you to do a job, so just figure it out.
- Are you here to bring me another problem?
- That's the worst idea I've ever heard.
- Can't you do anything right?
- What were you thinking?
- You're not very professional.
- The problem is you just don't get it.

- Just do what I tell you to do.
- Because I said so.
- That's a stupid idea.

Demeaning, condescending, or patronizing comments have four problems. First, they are disrespectful. Second, each of the comments is focused on the needs of the leader and not the needs of the employee. Third, the leader is not effectively communicating with the employee. Fourth, the employee is unlikely to forget these comments. People in our training sessions recall belittling and disrespectful comments with vivid clarity, even if the comments were made twenty or thirty years ago.

Believing Gossip and Rumors Instead of Facts

Unfair leaders make bad decisions based on gossip and third-party information that is not, or cannot, be verified. One new hire was told by a co-worker that the boss did not like him. Because he had been on the job less than 45 days, and his performance evaluation was not due for another month and a half, he wanted to clear the air. He went to his boss's office and asked if there was a problem. The boss said no.

The employee, in an effort to resolve the misunderstanding, asked if there was a performance problem. He was shocked when the boss pulled out a list of transgressions from showing up late to failure to complete training and an inability to get along with others. The employee asked for specific examples and, of course, the unfair boss had none. It turns out that one of the experienced workers was intensely jealous of the new hire's professional abilities and was trying to sabotage him by bad-mouthing him to the boss. It worked. As much as the new hire tried to fight the unfair allegations, the boss was convinced the accuser spreading rumors was right. The talented new hire quit one month later.

Comparing Apples to Oranges

One boss said to his direct report, "John, you are having a lot of problems with consistently achieving a customer satisfaction rating above 4.5 out of 5. I would like you to work with Larry and learn everything you can from him because our customers love Larry." John angrily responded, "Since you want me to be just like Larry, can I also come to work late each day? Can I also be paid Larry's salary?" Comparing one employee to another is like comparing one sibling to another; it seldom ends well. Everyone has both strengths and opportunities for improvement. The strategy may have been intended to motivate the employee but, instead, came across as unfair.

Performance Evaluations That are Late or Nonexistent

Employees, especially millennials, crave attention and feedback. The most formal feedback is the performance evaluation. We have heard every excuse a manager can make for why their performance reviews are late, just a form, or why they will not be doing them at all this year. Performance appraisals, when well done, are a formality of what the leader and employee already know. When the leader consistently provides helpful guidance, encouraging monitoring, and planning for career advancement, a meeting with the boss is something to look forward to instead of something to dread. Without regular attention, employees lack clarity regarding what they are doing well, as well as their opportunities for improvement. Employees are not sure what to focus on, whether or not their efforts are what the organization needs, or if they are contributing to the team's success.

Here is the reality. The employee gives their manager approximately 2070 hours of labor a year. When the manager cannot devote two to six hours of their time throughout the year to let the employee know their strengths, as well as their opportunities for development and growth, most employees will view that lack of effort on the part of the manager as unfair.

Prescription for Fair Success

Fairness impacts every aspect of leadership and requires a leader to put themselves into the shoes of others. Fairness reflects equality and not putting yourself above others based on rank. When leaders are unfair, they indirectly tell people that they do not value their relationship with those they are trying to lead. When people do not feel valued or respected, they rapidly lose their motivation to follow their leader.

The following actions will help you be a fair and consistent leader employees respect:

Be Honest

Most managers can tell you about the importance of being honest. But, great leaders know the only time they gain points for being fair and honest is when that honesty costs them something. When a leader is unhappy with employee performance, for instance, they know it is critical to communicate their concerns. A great leader may start off the conversation with "I know you may not be happy or agree with my feedback, but I think it's really important you are aware of my concerns with your performance." This practice of being honest, especially when it is difficult to be honest, is the fair and right thing to do. The practice of consistently being honest eliminates a lot of negative surprises that exist within relationships, teams, and organizations.

Selflessly Give Credit Where Credit Is Due

Great leaders know they, as the leader, played a role in the outcome when their teams perform well. Every great coach or quarterback being congratulated after a winning game immediately says "I am proud of the entire team," and "All the credit goes to the team."

> **Wins belong to the team.**

Confident leaders feel great about ensuring that praise and recognition are given to the team or the right people on the team. Humble leaders often feel uncomfortable with all the praise and credit being attributed to them as the leader, even when it is deserved. Effective leaders respond with "I need everyone on the senior team to know that I'm grateful for the compliments, but it's important you know my team deserves the credit and praise. They worked incredibly hard to achieve these amazing results. I'd be really grateful if someone on the senior team would send my team an email to let them know you are aware of their great work, and you are grateful for both their help and outstanding results."

Distinguish Among Your Employees

There is a distinction between fairness and consistency. Based on insights shared by Bill Catlette and Richard Hadden, authors of *Contented Cows MOOve Faster*, consistency means you treat everyone equally, at all times and in all situations. Fairness means you treat each of your team members uniquely, with equity, based on their preferences, needs, and varied contributions. Consistency makes no distinction based on individual team members' contributions or even lack of contribution. You interpret and follow the rules consistently, treating everyone the same. There is no flexibility, no exceptions, and no individual path. A machine could make the decisions because, when the variables are the same, the outcome is the same.

However, fairness is more discerning. It requires you to think, apply logic, and use sound judgment. Remember, treating people fairly is not the same as treating people the same. Different people need different motivations and styles of leadership, but the basis of the leader's behavior has to be based on being objective and fair. A fair leader recognizes not all team members need or deserve the same method of recognition, feedback, training, or mentoring. Joe Kraus, founder of Excite.com, a web portal, boldly states:

> *"Nothing demotivates people like the equal treatment of unequals. When you hire a bozo and treat him the same as a rock star, it deflates the rock star."*

In the real world, not everyone wins and gets a participation trophy. Your business is no different. If you have been clear about what success looks like and how it is measured, chances are some employees are hitting home runs again and again and some are barely meeting goals. Unfortunately, you will still have some who spend more time arguing the goals are unrealistic and unattainable than it would have taken to actually achieve the goal.

A fair leader provides more recognition and, when appropriate, rewards those who meet or exceed the goals. The whiners who do not meet the goal will cry "unfair" when there is no blanket recognition or reward for all team members. When this happens, know you are earning fairness points with those who count.

Coach and Mentor

A fair leader holds all employees accountable for clearly-defined performance standards. When an employee falls short, the leader invests time and energy to help the employee develop and find solutions for the performance challenge. If the employee exhibits a desire to learn and grow, the leader continues in this mentoring capacity. If, for whatever reason, however, the employee will not or cannot correct the problems despite having the tools they need, the leader has to make the tough decision to either let the employee go or transfer them to a more suitable position.

Be Consistent with Your Decisions

Team members want to work for a reliable and predictable leader. When searching for 360° feedback, a great question to ask is "Can my teammates consistently predict what decisions I will make in similar types of situations?" Fair leaders are consistent in how they approach solving problems and, ultimately, how they make decisions. If you use your personal and organizational values to guide your decisions, you are much more likely to be consistent and fair.

> *Fair leaders are consistent in how they approach solving problems and, ultimately, how they make decisions. If you use your personal and organizational values to guide your decisions, you are much more likely to be consistent and fair.*

Be Consistently Optimistic and Stable

As a leader, your job is to elevate the team's spirit, improve the team's condition and ultimately achieve the team's mission and goals. A moody leader is unfair to the team. Every time the boss is in a bad mood, it rubs off on others. It becomes a huge distraction for team members and disrupts their focus on achieving the goal. A second problem occurs when leaders stay in a bad mood because team members stop coming to them with information for fear of the unfair boss's reaction. Although leaders will eventually learn of the problems on their team, the information will be received after a significant delay. We all know every day may not be a GREAT day, but it is the job of a fair leader to be consistent in their mood and raise the spirits of their team. When the manager walks into the office, you should be able to feel the positive energy and optimism following them in.

Praise Publicly

Criticize or provide constructive feedback in one-on-one coaching sessions. Praise publicly. Always.

Treat Everyone with Respect

When I observe people treating others disrespectfully, I wonder, "Who raised these people?" Most people are raised by a combination of parents, family members, and communities. Most would agree that learning to treat people right is a necessary life skill. Treating people with respect should be a no-brainer. Great leaders not only treat people with respect and dignity, they hold others accountable for doing the same.

> *Great leaders not only treat people with respect and dignity, they hold others accountable for doing the same.*

One of our five golden CEO rules is "Treat everyone with the respect we award our best clients. Everyone." That includes the delivery people, the people who vacuum the floors, the new technicians, everyone. Good leaders take action against others and hold them accountable when they treat people poorly. We admired the CEO who made this abundantly clear to one of his managers we were coaching. "If you don't change the way you treat people in our company, you will not work here." That specific feedback let the manager know what was expected and motivated him to improve his behavior. The way you treat the gardener, hotel maid, or the janitor should be no different than the way you treat a sitting president. You can tell the quality of a leader by how they treat the people in their life who do not have the ability to impact their future.

Make Leadership Decisions Objectively

The Olympic trials are a great example of objectivity. It does not matter if you won six gold medals in the last Olympics. You will still have to try out again for the next Olympics to see if you are still competitive enough to represent your country. Are you still one of your country's fastest swimmers? Great, you make the team. If not, you know why.

Although there is a lot of subjectivity in leadership, the best leaders are able to rely on objective standards to back up their decisions. When an employee asks, "Why did you rate me a 'three' on the teamwork competency in this year's performance review?" the leader is able to back up their rating with objective examples. Better yet, the leader is able to explain exactly what the employee needs to do differently to achieve a "four" or "five" on the next performance review. This ensures that everyone has a fair chance to succeed.

Create Synergy

A strong leader understands their team is a blend of diverse talent, personalities, ethnic backgrounds, and sometimes just general quirkiness. The fair leader knows team members as individuals, respects their uniqueness, and treats people the way they want to be treated. The fair leader is able to synergize the group by doing so; often achieving phenomenal outcomes because people feel good about themselves and are motivated to go the extra mile.

Practice Forgiveness

Great leaders accept the reality that no one is perfect. Everyone makes mistakes. Effective leaders are quick to admit their own mistakes and let people know what they will do differently in the future. Fair leaders are quick to take responsibility for ensuring problems are corrected, and they are quick to offer forgiveness to the people who were responsible for the problem. Great leaders know people need them to have their back at all times, especially when things go wrong.

Welcome Feedback

Great leaders are humble, and they are good listeners. They welcome and accept feedback, even when they are sometimes accused of being unfair. They keep the lines of communication open with team members by asking questions and reflecting on the answers. It would be easier to interact only with the employees who enjoy telling you what you want to hear, but a fair leader knows they will not continue to grow and further develop as a leader without encouraging and being open to tough feedback. Being open to feedback also indicates to your team you are trying to be the best leader you can for the team and organization.

Practice Fairness

The only time managers will gain points for being fair is when it costs them something to be fair. The employee we discussed in the earlier example was the first to request her vacation and deserved to have it approved based on the existing policy. The problem for the manager was she wanted the employees who performed the best and she liked the most to get the best vacation. Approving the vacation request—based on her own policy—would have been the fair thing to do. But, doing so would have made some of her best performing employees unhappy. There are some days your closest associates may not be happy with your "fair" business decisions. However, these are the times everyone will remember that, while they may not be happy with your decision, they do work for a consistent and fair leader.

Being a fair leader takes courage, wisdom, people smarts, and a whole lot of good judgment. Being fair is tough, but fair leaders achieve better results, have greater employee loyalty and retention, and top the charts in respect. Being consistent and treating everyone the same is easy, but the easy route will not get you, or your team, as far.

7 Tips for Fair Leadership

1. As a leader, your job is to elevate team spirit, improve the team's condition, and, ultimately, achieve the team's mission and goals.
2. Be consistent with your standards, decisions, and moods.
3. Praise in public, criticize in private. Always.
4. Treat everyone with the utmost respect and hold others accountable for doing the same.
5. Give the team credit for all wins.
6. Back your people when they make honest mistakes.
7. Create a workplace where everyone believes they can succeed.

5

They Don't Understand We Are One Team

Talent wins games, but teamwork and intelligence wins championships.

—Michael Jordan

Two executives blamed each other for late deliveries, budget overruns, project problems, and poor communication. They were quick to point the finger at the other when problems arose. Both managers ambitiously aspired to be promoted to the next level in the organization, and they both believed they had the skills necessary to advance. Both executives also believed that, if they could be the other's boss, all problems would be solved. They could tell the other executive what to do and use their position and power to force compliance. Repeated attempts by upper management to get them to work cooperatively failed.

In another organization, an executive wanted to be promoted to COO. She proposed several recommendations to change the organizational structure so more and more departments reported to her, thereby expanding her role. The problem was that her recommendations were obviously self-serving and did not make organizational sense. One team member described her as self-centered, power-hungry, and mean-spirited.

In another company, the new executive was in the first 100 days on the job, and he was failing. Why? He was invisible to his people. He took over and they barely saw him. He didn't walk around and get to know his team. He didn't know where their offices were. His office door was open, but he was never there when his managers stopped by. He made a cursory showing at a few official events, but he did not speak with anyone who worked for him. He was too busy chatting with the other vice presidents and the CEO.

His team noticed his lack of time with them and felt he did not care about anyone but himself. As a result, less than three months after he took over, his people dismissed him as one of those bosses who is more worried about his own career than helping his people. He lost the respect of his team, and subsequently, productivity declined.

In each of the above scenarios, the executives failed as leaders because they did not take the necessary time and actions to build a united team. In two of these examples, the CEO also dropped the ball by not taking quick action to ensure every executive reporting to her was committed to working as a cohesive unit. When a leader fails to quickly deal with team members who are disruptive or not loyal and committed to the team, the situation gets worse.

The first time many of us work as a team is in school on a "group project." Most of us learned

- No one else is going to work as hard as me.
- No one else does any work.
- No one else can be trusted.

With this introduction to working with others, it is no wonder many people claim they would rather work alone.

Team members complain

- I don't like the other people on my team.
- I don't like the project.
- I'm not valued.
- I do all the work.
- The person in charge is incompetent.

Most supervisors and managers agree there have been times in their careers when they were unable to build a united team. For various reasons, the team did not come together. These supervisors and managers were all quick to rationalize why their groups did not perform as a team. Some common excuses included

- Team members lack commitment.
- The long-term employees are more comfortable working independently.
- Some people refuse to change and work with others.
- The employees and/or the organization tried teaming up before and it did not work.
- Upper management sends messages that encourage teams, but their non-supportive actions speak louder than their words.
- The team has one, two, or more people that others don't want to work with.
- It takes more time to accomplish something as a team than it does working alone.
- No one on the team is accountable.
- The team has politically-based membership rather than performance-based membership.

- People who telework and other non-traditional workers, such as independent contractors, are "never around."
- The team has low goals or expectations.
- Team members (and occasionally, the leader) stopped caring.

What is missing from this list of excuses is *lack of leadership.*

Path to Failure

Every player on every professional football, baseball, basketball, and soccer team knows team leadership is the basis for the success or failure of the team as a whole. Why do so many leaders fail to build a cohesive team?

Failing to Clarify and Communicate a Compelling Vision with Clear Goals

When a team does not have a clear vision, purpose, or goals, they have no clear direction to work toward. Most likely, some of those actions will undermine the team's ability to function as a united workgroup.

Not Holding All Team Members Equally Accountable for Results

When the vision and goals for the team are clear, it is easier to know what actions team members should take and for what results they will be held accountable. When leaders do not hold team members accountable for producing the desired results, the effectiveness of both the individuals and the team decline. But, effectiveness is not the only thing that declines. Morale will also decline because the employees who are accountable begin to resent team members who are not pulling their weight. Worse, the highest performing employees begin to question why they should go out of their way to produce great work when there are no benefits for superior work and no consequences for poor performance.

Not Enforcing Team Loyalty

When you are a member of an executive team, your primary loyalty is to that team, and not to the operational team for which you are responsible, which sounds counter intuitive. Many leaders feel strongly their first loyalty should be to the people who work for them. Well, yes; however, when the executive team makes a decision, every member of that team needs to ensure they uphold the decision *as though it was their own idea* and turn the goal into a reality. This is sometimes a challenge for leaders when members of their own team do not like or agree with the executive team's decisions. When executives commit to the executive team's decision, and then do not hold their own teams accountable for implementing the outcomes, there is a lack of loyalty to the primary team and the organization. When executives do not hold other executive members accountable to the primary team, the leaders and the organization's effectiveness diminishes significantly.

Not Effectively Dealing with Conflict

When leaders do not effectively deal with conflict among team members, the conflict and hurt among team members worsens. When this happens, team members lose respect for the leader, and teamwork deteriorates. If the situation continues long enough, the best team members will leave.

Not Seeing Each Other Face to Face

It's important to note that dysfunctional teams do anything and everything humanly possible to avoid having meetings. Team members on a dysfunctional team love to cajole their leaders, "We are really busy this week. Can we cancel the meeting?" If leaders take the advice of the team members, it will work in the short term, but in the long term, it is usually a disaster. Consistent meetings promote better communication, improved collaboration, and increased awareness of how everyone's role contributes to the team's success.

The last thing a team member of a dysfunctional team wants to do is be held accountable while sitting across the table from someone they are in a conflict with or do not like. Some leaders believe the solution for conflict is to avoid it. They stop holding meetings because there are conflicts on the team.

> *Ignoring conflict does not resolve conflict.*

If the team does not get together, then the conflict remains an issue. By not meeting and dealing with the disagreements, the leader of the team guarantees the conflicts will not be resolved. Eventually, all the people who do not get along will have only one thing in common ... they will not respect the leader.

Directing Individuals versus a Team

Some leaders believe they have a team because they gather the people together once a month, and everyone reports what they are working on. There is no teamwork, collaboration, or dialogue with each other, just reports. This is not a team and it will not operate as such. Committees have members, but working together is not a requisite as long as each committee member does their respective job. This is how many companies operate.

Teams collaborate by working together, struggling together, brainstorming together, and helping each other. They create bigger successes than individuals can achieve on their own.

Lacking the Ability to Get the Team to Work Cross-Departmentally

Some leaders are great at building and leading successful teams. What they lack is the ability to use those same skills to effectively promote teamwork with other departments and leaders in the organization. These leaders fail to recognize that to be successful and promotable, they need to not only do a great job with their own team, they also need to build strong relationships and enhance teamwork throughout the organization.

We worked with a manufacturing company. The first stage job was to cut pieces of glass. The second stage was to refine the glass plates, which often included several rounds of re-cutting. We realized if the first stage team altered their cuts by half an inch, it would reduce the second stage re-cutting process. However, the first stage team didn't want to. Why? This team made their quotas with less work when they did it their way. Even though altering their process would reduce overall work and increase profits, cross-departmental cooperation was neither encouraged nor rewarded.

Not Communicating to the Entire Team

When leaders do not promote intra-departmental communication and prefer to communicate one-on-one, information is not shared equally, and teamwork suffers. One team member noted, in an assessment, her boss had a policy that dictated she would "only communicate with you on a need-to-know basis." As a result, team members operated with limited information. Some team members didn't know what the rest of the department was working on so they could not help, nor could they ask for or receive help from others.

Prescription for Team Building Success

The prescription for success in teamwork begins by understanding what makes a great team.

In our consulting practices and research, we uncovered six characteristics that great teams have in common.

A clear and compelling vision of what they are trying to accomplish. Someone on the team, either the supervisor, manager, or other team member conveys a positive vision of the team's purpose and over-arching goals. On a consulting project with a manufacturing company, a cross-departmental group of people came together to improve the quality of one of the organization's new products. It was evident at the first meeting that three members of the team really believed management had empowered them to solve the problems. Although there was some cynicism from two team members, the strong belief from the three members that this team really could have a positive impact was enough to win over the cynics and get all team members committed to solving the problem together.

Your vision of your team's future will have a significant impact on your team. Whether a manager's vision is positive, neutral or negative, it is important to remember the manager usually takes the respective actions that prove their vision right.

Shared goals. Team members are equally committed to a common purpose, goals, and a working approach for which they hold themselves mutually accountable. As a supervisor or manager, you have the opportunity to set the goals for your team, or better, with the team. Either way, it is the responsibility of the leader to ensure the members of their team know what must be accomplished.

If the team does not buy into the goal and make a commitment to accomplish the task, there is a large chance the project will either not be completed or not be completed correctly. As a leader, there are times when someone higher than you in management or a customer will dictate a goal to you, e.g., we need 200 units shipped by Friday. In this case, as the extended arm of management, you often do not have a choice. The task has to be completed.

How can leaders create a shared goal? First, ask the team if this is something they think they can accomplish by Friday. If team members say "no," the appropriate questions include, "What would we have to do, or what do we need to do differently, to accomplish this goal?" One team member offered that, if they could get the products from another internal department one half day earlier, it would be tough, but they would be able to accomplish the production. The leader was able to get the other department to provide the products four hours earlier, and the shared goal was accomplished on time.

As the leader, you have to ask and discover team concerns and objections about problems that get in the way of achieving the goal. You cannot assume the goal is a shared one just because you communicated to the group what needed to happen.

Driven by performance challenges. It is the challenge that energizes a team to greatness, regardless of its location in the organization. Have you ever watched an interview where someone is characterized as the underdog? Being told that something is close to impossible makes people want to prove naysayers wrong. A common set of demanding performance goals, a significant accomplishment that needs to be completed, or a large problem to be solved can result in an outcome of both high performance and a stronger team. Teams thrive on performance challenges; they produce mediocre results without them.

Knowing the "Why." Almost every large organization can share horror stories about how teams have orchestrated one type of team disaster or another. In many of these situations, team members did not understand "why" teams were being formed. When there is a question of "why," you can guarantee some team members will feel the team's task or goal does not make sense or will not contribute to the organization's success. As a supervisor or manager, you need to ensure your team is working on a challenging goal that is meaningful to each member of the team.

Value and respect for the contributions of each member. Team members need to recognize each individual brings a unique gift or contribution to the team. It is important each team member recognizes it would be harder to accomplish the task without each individual's unique contribution. That doesn't mean everyone will love everyone else on the team, but everyone must be valued and respected. We have observed instances where appreciation for others may not transcend outside the workplace. For example, a supervisor stated to us his most valuable technician was not someone he would spend time with off the job. Their personalities were very different, but the supervisor made sure we knew "when it comes to producing high-quality parts and solving big problems, this person is the best!"

Great teams win. It doesn't matter whether you are on a sports team or a team in a business environment—great teams accomplish their goals and tasks. It is your challenge as a supervisor or manager to build a winning team.

Anyone can win by being given ideal, perfect employees to do the job. The problem is that, in real life, this never happens. And if it did happen, there would be no need for the supervisor!

In reality, most times we get a diverse mixture of talent, skills, knowledge, and abilities in our people. A few may fall into the ideal/perfect employee category. The majority will perform as "middle-of-the-road" employees. They may not seem ideal/perfect, but they are not challenging you as the leader either. Happily, most supervisors have only a few truly terrible and difficult employees. These are the people who are so difficult you find yourself lying awake at 3:00 a.m. thinking, "Why do they have to report to me?"

It is important to understand challenging employees are not always bad employees. These are the people who help you strengthen your leadership skills. As you navigate your way through managing these challenges, remember the individual's value and contribution to the team. When difficult employees internalize the vision and common goals, they have the ability to advance to a middle-of-the-road or ideal employee.

Leaders need to develop the ability to leverage this blending of people and talents: formulate a positive vision; set challenging, shared goals; clarify roles; set deadlines; and build value and respect for each team member's contribution.

Team members should feel as though they can do their work better as part of a team rather than working on the project individually. They should feel as though the team working together is going to accomplish more than what any one team member could do by themselves. When this happens, the team's chances of winning increases tremendously.

How to Build Great Teams

What do great leaders do to succeed in building great teams? The following eight strategies help leaders build great teams.

Step Up and Be the Leader

Do you remember being assigned a group project in school? Most of the time, there was no clear team leader; there was little accountability; and the person who cared the most about their grade in that class did the most work. We learned working on teams often meant unfairness—we were going to have to do more of our share than we might have to do if we were working individually.

This was how we were taught to work on teams in school. It is no wonder there is conflict, misunderstandings, and lack of clear direction when working on teams in the workplace. Successful leaders step up and ensure the goals and roles are clear and team members are held accountable for the team's success.

The reality is we are better together. That explains why people gather together to live in communities, brainstorm on projects, and are drawn to each other in social situations. The leader's challenge is some people enjoy working with certain team members more than others. Not everyone knows how to work well in teams, and it is the leader's job to make that happen.

Lean into Conflict

Strong leaders understand conflict is inevitable, and disagreements can be healthy and productive when dealt with correctly. Resolving conflict means discussing the difficult issues and bringing everyone involved together to reach an understanding. Conflict that is effectively dealt with by the leader can actually serve to build a stronger foundation.

In some cases, when leaders do not immediately resolve conflict, it is helpful to bring in a consultant to help them work through the issues. Otherwise, those issues can threaten to destroy morale, the mission, and the team.

Deal Quickly with Behaviors that Undermine the Team

Most people consider themselves above-average drivers, but statistically, that isn't possible. Many people pride themselves on working harder than everyone else. Many people think they are smarter than others on the team. The reality is that many people have blinders on when it comes to their own work performance and their ability to be a successful team member.

It is challenging, therefore, for a manager to harness multiple, and sometimes (very) strong, personalities into a cohesive team when there are people who clearly do not want to adhere to the same standards of behavior they expect of others. You have probably heard someone scoff, "Rules are for other people!" These people expect the rules to apply to everyone else but them, and they are frequently the most difficult to manage.

Sometimes, these "quarterbacks" who want to call all the plays are your most valuable talent. They are usually out-of-the-box thinkers, and they excel when they are the star of the team or when they operate alone. But, when they refuse to lend themselves to the overall wellbeing of the team, their actions are distracting and counterproductive.

Some people work better as individuals than they do with a team. As one leader we were coaching commented, "I don't really care about the team's goals. All I want to know is what I am accountable for." This leader's attitude was not supportive of the overall team, and team members felt his lack of support. How do you effectively handle problem team members?

Address Problems Right Away

As a manager, as soon as you discover someone is violating his or her boundaries, not contributing, or working contrary to team goals, pull him or her in for a meeting. Explain that the motivation for the action may be right, but working outside the legal or safety parameters or the values of the organization or not supporting others on the team is detrimental to the team's overall mission.

Frequently, these employees do not understand the strategic picture. They do not have all the facts, and they do not understand the unintended consequences of their decisions. When providing feedback or what Marshall Goldsmith describes as "feed forward" (more positive and proactive), reactions will differ, but many may fall into one of these common response scenarios:

Denial—"I didn't mean to." The deficient team member's action may stem from pure carelessness, neglect, laziness, or sheer lack of knowledge, which indicates a need for more training.

Your solution: Ask the person to discuss it right away. Call him on what happened and ask questions to ensure he understands the effect that his behavior has on others. "That may not have been your intent, but when you were late with your products on Friday, the next team couldn't process the order, and we lost it." Ask the employee what he will do differently to make sure the undesired action doesn't happen again.

Questions like these put the burden of thinking of a solution on the employee. Help him see the consequences as well as how he can figure out the solution. Make this conversation a coaching session and a training opportunity.

Defensive—"I don't see why it is a problem." The team member doesn't see why he created a problem because he does not have the maturity, the wisdom, the facts, the experience, or the reasoning ability to discern the real issue. Sometimes employees refuse to see they are at fault. These team members try to argue their way out of trouble.

Your solution: "This action (be specific) wound up costing $___ and __ of extra time because this outcome was not achieved ___ (again, be specific.) Ask your defensive employee, "Do you see this as a problem?" When you gain agreement there is a problem, you can then ask for their solutions to solve the problem. The defensive responders tend to be experts at deflecting the issue. Managers may hear, "But Charlie does it all the time!" or some other excuse that has little to do with the current problem. Don't let your defensive team member lead you off topic. Stay focused on the current problem by asking the team member another good question: "Is it possible I also meet with Charlie one-on-one to discuss performance-related issues?" Answer your own question, "I do. So, I want to ask you again, what are you going to do differently to ensure this problem is not repeated?"

Put the responsibility of fixing the problem back on them. Ask questions to help them find the right solution that corrects the mistake and provides a real learning experience. If they don't have to work to fix the negative consequences, the behavior or problem will likely be repeated. These people need more attention, follow-up, and supervision.

Apologetic—"I'm sorry. This is all my fault." This is the easiest response to deal with, if it is sincere. If this attitude is genuine, you can move forward quickly.

Your solution: "Thanks for taking responsibility. How are you going to take care of it so the problem never happens again?" Chances are, they already have a solution in mind as soon as they realize the problem. Assure them you consider the matter resolved and you intend to move forward.

Personalization—"This is because you don't like me." The response is much like the defensive response. The team member may try to use something personal as an excuse to not see the behavior. Stay focused!

Your solution: Phrase the problem using a third-party. "If Frank needed some help on this project, how should he best approach you?" Have them explain and then delve into the problem. "Well, Frank asked you on Tuesday and you promised help by Wednesday, but it didn't happen, so now we are all behind. What do you think Frank should do? What do you think you might do differently to help Frank complete his projects?" Ask plenty of open-ended questions that focus on the issue in a non-blaming manner, and then close it with consensual agreement. "Are you willing to help Frank so you can get this finished by Friday? Let's go talk with him together and schedule the rest of the project."

Bite the Bullet

Sometimes, however, you as a leader do everything right, and the bad attitude and poor performance continues. You may have to consider whether that person, however gifted, is the wrong fit for the team. If you have done everything possible to elicit his talents and adequately trained him to work with others, then you shouldn't feel as though you have failed if it's time to help them find another job. Some people need to get off the bus so the bus can get to where it needs to go. Any coach will attest that great players are valuable only when they contribute to the betterment of the team.

Keep Yourself on Track—Be Accountable to Your Team and Yourself

Accepting accountability means not making excuses and not shifting blame. Positively stated, being accountable means taking responsibility for ensuring your team produces the results they are hired to produce. As a leader, you are committed, accountable, and responsible for all losses and profits, all mistakes and achievements, failures and successes. You make the decisions that are crucial to the success of your business, department, division, or staff, and you are personally accountable for the sustainability of your work.

Be accountable to yourself, for yourself. Set expectations for what you want to accomplish.

Set goals and milestones as you would for an employee. Establish timelines. Most people work best when they have a deadline so give yourself clear goals and a timeframe for achievement. Put yourself on a daily, weekly, and monthly schedule for outcomes and results. The team will be more productive when you work not only as the leader of the people you supervise but also as a player who adds significant value to the team.

Be a Great Team Player

Yes, you as a leader manage teams. But you are part of a larger organization as well. What are you doing to make sure you are a great team player? Being part of a team means bringing your willingness to change, perspective, adaptability, and skills to what the team needs.

Lead Your Team Out of a Crisis

From time to time, every supervisor or manager will find they are in charge of a team in crisis. Crises come in many shapes and sizes. A few of the crises we have seen supervisors struggle with include team members who do not get along; company financial problems; morale or motivation at an all-time low; quality problems; customer service problems; departments at war with each other; and top management not being supportive of a team or department.

The deeper the crisis, the more challenging it is for supervisors and managers to figure out how to solve the problems and put the team back on track. Many times, supervisors and managers do not know what action they should take. Many possible actions seem to have the potential to send the team into a deeper crisis. Because of this risk, some opt for no action, in the "hopes" the situation will get better on its own. Very seldom does the team come out of a crisis on its own when the supervisor or manager relies on "hope." The following action steps will help you lead your team out of a crisis:

Face reality. When a crisis hits and supervisors/ managers are not sure what to do, the first inclination is to deny the problem is as big as it really is. If we bury our heads in the sand, the problem will not seem as large. But, when we stick our heads in the sand, we leave other parts of our body exposed. Face reality. The problem, most likely, will not go away unless you do something to solve the crisis.

Take action. If you wait until your boss helps to solve the problem or until team members decide to help solve the problem, you may wait forever. Supervisors and managers who do not take action to solve team problems are not doing their jobs. Be empowered. You have the ability to take responsibility for making decisions and taking actions that will lead the team from crisis. If you are not empowered to do this, then there is a good chance your team will remain in crisis.

Prioritize. When teams fall into a crisis, there are usually many problems that may impact the team. You cannot fix all the problems at once so it is in your best interest to get the team involved and prioritize the actions that need to be taken. If the team is unwilling to prioritize actions, then you will have to decide which problems to solve and in what order.

Focus on results. When teams are in crisis, there is a tendency to focus on trying to fix the relationships that have broken down. While the intention is good, we have found it is much more productive for floundering teams to focus on results. When everyone is focused on the purpose of the team and the results it must produce, many of the relationship problems will resolve on their own. If the team is not productive, there will always be relationship struggles.

Recruit the cream of the crop. During a crisis, it is often the very best team members who leave. They join other departments or will find a new job with another company. Unfortunately, the most challenging team members never seem to leave. They would much rather tell everyone how bad things are than to do anything to change the situation. In a crisis, analyze your people assets and spend time asking the top performers to band with you and help solve the problems. Most people will stay in a bad situation if they know they can help improve the crisis, feel valued, and have a positive vision that tomorrow will be better than today.

Praise and recognize your people often. The reason we emphasize this as a specific point is because, when a team goes into crisis mode and you are the leader of this team, you may focus your energy on what is going wrong instead of recognizing the things that are going right. When people do not feel valued, and the team or organization is in a crisis, team members start to say, "I don't get paid enough to put up with this crap." One way we can minimize this feeling in our team members is to value their contributions and recognize them for doing things right.

Tighten discipline. When teams go into crisis, there are usually many things happening that are not conducive to good teamwork. For example, we might find members coming to work late, people coming to meetings late or not coming at all, work being completed with inferior quality, internal customer service lacking between departments, and people not taking responsibility to solve problems. When a crisis occurs, it is in your best interest as a supervisor or manager to tighten, not loosen discipline. This means you need to hold people accountable for coming to work on time or producing quality parts. Not doing so sends the message to team members that negative behaviors are acceptable.

Identify who is responsible and what role that individual will play. In a moment of crisis, it is critical that you clarify who will be taking responsibility for leading the team out of crisis. This point helps to keep focus on the results. When a team is in crisis, you will usually find team members are clear on what is wrong and who is to blame, but they are not clear on what needs to be done and who is responsible. As the supervisor, you can assign roles and responsibilities.

Over-communicate. When a supervisor or manager is in over his or her head with team problems, there is a tendency to focus energy on operational, rather than leadership, tasks. You may mutter, "All I do around here is put out fires." As a supervisor, your primary role is to support others. Increase your communication with team members: information provided by you and information communicated to you by the team. Most of the time, your team has the ability to solve the problems if you utilize them as a resource. Increasing your communication will lessen the negative impact of the crisis.

Maintain a positive mental attitude. If you throw in the towel because you feel the situation is hopeless, then your team members will likely adopt a similar mentality. Not having a positive mental attitude can have a negative impact on a supervisor's or manager's career. If you have no hope of the situation getting better but someone else on the team or in the organization does, then your team members will begin to follow someone else. A supervisor or manager with no followers is not a leader.

A caveat: We are the first to agree—teams are not for everyone or every situation. Nonetheless, teams usually outperform other groups or individuals, and teams perfect individual members' strengths and overcome their weaknesses. We are better when we work together.

7 Tips for Building a Great Team

1. Collaborate to create a team vision of the team's purpose and desired outcome.
2. Set clear, challenging goals and then clarify the roles of team members.
3. Hold team members accountable for the desired results.
4. Lean into conflict. Deal with behaviors that undermine the success of the team.
5. Value and recognize the team's success and individual team members' contributions.
6. Hold consistent meetings that add value for each member of the team.
7. Be a great team leader and a great team player. Play the right role at the right time and lead the team to a win!

6

They Want To Be Miss Congeniality

I used to care a lot that people liked me. That's no longer as much the case. Of course, nobody wants not to be liked, but I don't care as much. I remember feeling liberated when it no longer influenced my decision-making.

—Deborah Bial

The truth is, we all want to be liked on some level. Some leaders' desire to be liked is so strong it overrides their need to be respected in the workplace. They want to be the leader, but they also want to be buddies with their subordinates. This is a recipe for disaster.

Do You Want to Win a Popularity Contest or Run a Company?

A CEO was hired from outside the company to take over for a retiring, experienced, and iron-fisted leader. With the outgoing CEO, everyone in the organization knew exactly where they stood on every issue. He was bluntly direct with his feedback and everyone was crystal clear on what he wanted.

The incoming CEO had never served in a chief executive role. In his previous organization, he had served as the CFO for ten years. He was technically brilliant, supremely organized, and very pleasant. He's the kind of guy you want for a neighbor. Unfortunately, eighteen months into his term as CEO, the Board asked for his resignation. He wanted everyone to agree on every issue and didn't want to make decisions that upset anyone. Every decision he made was focused on making his employees happy instead of making them effective.

> *When leaders place a high value on making everyone happy, they sacrifice good decisions.*

When leaders place a high value on making everyone happy, they sacrifice good decisions. Instead of making an employee temporarily unhappy by holding them accountable, this CEO repeatedly tolerated poor performance because he did not wish to upset his employees. He thought the solution to a complaining employee was to transfer them to another division, thereby "passing the trash." The problem now belonged to someone else, but was still no closer to a resolution.

In another example, the CEO designed an organizational structure focused around the happiness of his employees instead of creating an organizational structure that made functional sense and was in the best interest of the organization. To compound his problems, his high need to please others resulted in telling everyone what they wanted to hear. He told different versions of every story, depending on who he was talking to. This CEO was a really likeable guy. He was so likeable he ended up losing his job. As a leader, you have a choice. You can either be a great boss or you can shoot for the title of Miss Congeniality. You cannot do both.

The need to be liked and the fear of being disliked make us human. We love happy employees. When we work with leaders, our goal is always to create a workplace where people love to come to work. But, happy employees and thriving workplace cultures are not the result of leaders who

> *Happy employees and thriving workplace cultures are not the result of leaders who spend their time pleasing everyone.*

spend their time pleasing everyone. Instead, they are the result of strong leaders who are willing to make tough decisions that are in the best interest of the organization. We're not talking about being a bully. We're not talking about creating a toxic environment in which everyone lives in fear. As we said in previous chapters, such an environment is counterproductive. What we're talking about are leaders who lose their influence and their focus because being popular is their most important goal.

> *If only we'd stop trying to be happy we could have a pretty good time.*
>
> —Edith Wharton

When a leader has a pressing need to be liked by their employees and peers, there will be a negative impact on the level of respect for the leader and the results the leader achieves.

Path to Failure

There are many reasons leaders fail to make the right decisions that are rooted in a fear of not being liked or making employees unhappy—and just as many consequences associated with the decisions that result.

Wanting to Belong

Some leaders are highly motivated by a sense of belonging and being considered a true member of the team. They believe someone who belongs and is considered on the "inside" surely knows the culture of the organization and will make the right decisions.

This problem is especially prevalent when people are promoted from within. One day you are office mates, griping about the boss over lunch, and the next day you are the boss. That change in responsibilities is accompanied by a significant change in interpersonal dynamics.

We worked with a new leader who joined a team with a long history of not holding employees accountable. Instead of setting clear goals, clarifying expectations and holding her new team accountable for the desired results, she decided not to rock the boat and allowed the lack of accountability to continue. She wanted to "see where things went" before making any changes. Although she was well-liked for really understanding the culture of the team, there was little respect for her as a leader.

We also see this with very junior managers who want to demonstrate they are part of the team. In an effort to be liked, they interact with their subordinates in a casual manner. What they forget is their subordinates never forget their buddy-buddy boss has the power to fire them. This is a relationship that is not on equal ground, and it is not a friendship. "Familiarity breeds contempt" is how the military often describes the result of these interactions.

Wanting to Be Liked Before They Are Trusted

Some leaders mistakenly believe that to be trusted, you need to be liked. This is a paradox. It is possible to trust and respect someone you do not like. However, it is almost impossible to respect someone you do not trust. Leaders build trust and respect by making sound decisions that are in the best interests of the organization and the team. As every great leader has learned the hard way, not every team member will agree with your decisions, and not every team member is going to like you.

Designing an Organizational Structure Based on Personalities, Not Functionalities

A leader concerned with how her reports will feel about a new organizational structure floats the proposed changes to her direct reports in one-on-one meetings. Even though the new structure makes practical sense and is the right thing to do organizationally, two of her direct reports tell her they refuse to report to the proposed boss and demand they continue reporting to the CEO. Not wanting to upset these two direct reports, the CEO backs down from implementing the new structure.

Everyone wants access to the CEO, and everyone wants to directly report to the CEO. It makes people feel important to have the ear of the person at the top. Having 36 people reporting to the CEO, however, decreases the CEO's effectiveness. While it may hurt some people's feelings to no longer report directly to the big boss, the efficiency of the organization has to take precedence. When a leader places more weight on personalities than functionalities, the effectiveness of the organizational structure is severely undermined.

Not Understanding the "J" Curve of Change

Whenever a change is made, there's a good chance things will get worse before they get better. It's what we refer to as riding the "J" curve of change.

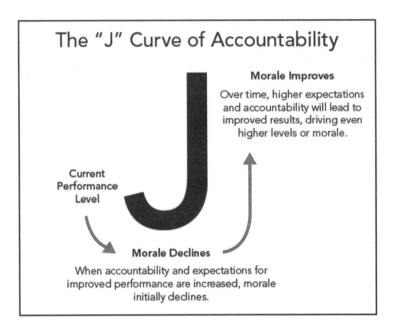

When you begin to hold employees accountable for implementing a change, remember that morale and productivity may go down before it comes back up and rises to a higher level. When you implement a change and hold employees accountable for the results, some employees may become resentful. Remember the "J" curve and keep pushing forward, even if some employees don't like you or the change. Many leaders, when facing resistance, back down, hesitate, or slow the implementation in an effort to solidify consensus. This is the wrong course. As people get used to the change, results will improve with the right leadership.

Not Wanting to Let Team Members Go

We worked with a leader whose boss was ready to fire him for failing to achieve the expected results. As executive coaches, we stressed to this leader that his job was at stake and asked, "What is preventing you from achieving the results your boss is holding you accountable for?"

The frustrated leader told us, "The employees are not capable of accomplishing these goals." Not capable is a powerful indictment. After inquiring further, we discovered the manager had taken many of the right steps to help his employees succeed. He had provided training and coaching for the employees, and, in desperation, took work away from the employees and completed it himself.

The goals were not unreasonable and they were still not being met. The right course of action was to replace the employees with people who were qualified, capable, and motivated to do the job. When we asked the manager why he had not taken the necessary action, he responded he did not want to hurt the employee's feelings by firing them, or upset the other long-term employees. He feared these changes would lead to unhappy employees, who might possibly quit. His fear of making his own employees unhappy was greater than his fear of losing his own job.

Wanting to Base Promotions on the Desires of Employees Rather than the Needs of the Organization

Do the people on your team have the vision, experience, capability, and passionate desire to take your team or organization to the next level? An even tougher question for a leader to ask is, "Do I have the vision, experience, capability, and passionate desire to take my team or organization to the next level?" If the answer to either question is no, you need to look outside your department or organization for qualified talent that will help take your team or organization to the next level. The challenge lies in the fact that, when you turn to the outside to fill a position, someone inside will not be happy with your decision. In fact, there is a good chance you will be faced with critical comments, such as

- "You do not value long-term employees."
- "You don't understand how things are done around here. We take care of our people."
- "You want to bring in someone new who will fire the people who built this company."

The decision to hire from outside the organization is especially difficult when existing team members feel they are more than qualified to take the position. Sometimes they are right, and sometimes they are not. As a leader, your hiring and promotion decisions need to be in the best interest of the team and organization and not affected by the feelings of your current employees.

Playing the "I've got a Secret" Game

Everyone wants to be "in the know," but leaders have to avoid discussing information or ideas with people that could have a negative impact on others if the information was made public. Leaders also have to be wary of sharing rumors or partial information that will result in people guessing at the truth. Sharing incomplete information will also result in employees not trusting their leader as sources of good information.

In the example where our leader wanted to realign the organizational chart, she told her direct reports she was just considering the changes and was not 100 percent certain she would implement the new structure. That turned into a problem when the news inevitably got out. She did end up moving forward with the changes and told the direct reports she was closest to. She did not inform the direct reports who would be most significantly impacted by the change until one hour before she sent out an official email announcement to all employees in the company. In this case, the leader was zero for two; the direct reports were unhappy with her decision and they did not respect her for the way the decision was implemented.

Working Around the Chain of Command to Avoid Potential Disagreements

More and more companies have adopted a "flat" system of reporting, where corporate hierarchy is "flattened" so people have more peers and few bosses. Successful organizations still have to have decision-makers and leaders. Clarity in knowing who reports to whom is about accountability, not personal power plays. People need to know who they are supposed to go to for information and who is responsible for the implementation of which projects. There are valid reasons for organizational charts, even if they seem outdated in today's workforce composed of an increasing number of contractors, part-time workers, and teleworkers. The responsibility for getting the job done doesn't change even if the workplace structure does.

> *When leaders bypass other leaders, it undermines authority.*

We coached a CEO who habitually bypassed his Chief Information Officer and went directly to the CIO's direct reports when he needed information or had a task that needed completion. His stated justification for doing so stemmed from a fear of conflict with the CIO. Instead of risking the CIO saying his request was "not a priority" or would have to wait, the CEO, instead, went directly to the employee he knew would eventually be responsible for the task. The CEO thought he was being friendly and efficient and "connecting" with employees. What the CEO was actually doing was undercutting the effectiveness of his CIO by going to the subordinates. The direct reports were uncomfortable with the situation and told their CIO about the CEO's requests. Directly or indirectly, the CEO was tacitly implying he didn't trust the

CIO. When he understood the gravity of bypassing the hierarchy, he brought everyone together, explained what he had done, apologized for not following his own structure, and the team was able to move forward.

Avoiding Conflict

Two team members don't like each other nor do they support each other's decisions. Instead of bringing the two team members together and resolving the conflict, the leader with a high need to be liked ignores the problem. He does not want to be associated with the conflict so he allows the conflict to continue. "It will get better," he tells himself. Almost always, the conflict gets worse. Although most people in this situation find it easier to avoid the other individual and not talk about the issues, respect for the leader deteriorates in the eyes of everyone on the team when the leader does not resolve conflicts that impact the effectiveness of the team.

Prescription for Respected Success

Strong leaders treat everyone well, but their actions are focused on the organization's mission, vision, and goals rather than getting everyone to like them.

Earn Respect

Although it is critical that a leader's focus be on building relationships based on respect rather than likeability, a balance between the two is necessary to be successful. Respect and likeability aside, we assume that a leader is competent enough to perform in the position they hold. If they are not adequately competent, they will never be respected, even if they are well liked. When the

> *It is more important to be respected than liked.*

foundation of competence has been established, balance comes into play. The diagram illustrates the role balance plays in being liked and/or respected.

The "sweet spot" in the diagram above is where leaders ideally want to be. These leaders are respected and liked for their ability to help their teams and organizations win. If circumstances put the sweet spot out of your reach, however, it is more important to be respected than liked.

There is some flexibility in the exact location of your particular sweet spot. Generally, leaders fall anywhere from 5-8 on the likability scale and 8-10 on the respect and results scale. Some leaders can dip to a 4 on the likeability scale, and with great results and respect, will survive and do fine. And, of course, great leaders understand there will be days some people (or a lot of people) will not agree with or like anything they do.

A lethal combination is a workforce that does not like

nor respect its leader, and the leader has a reputation for producing poor results.

If you are a leader who rates low on both likeability and results, do not be surprised if your most highly motivated and talented team members do not like or respect you. If everyone on the team has negative feelings towards you, they will unite around a common vision and goal. The vision is to save themselves from the ineffective leader who has absolutely no grounds to be liked. Sometimes the situation gets so bad that the team takes collective action to get the leader fired.

Clarify and Crystalize Your Personal Leadership Vision

In chapter one, we talked about the importance of having a compelling vision for the organization and a solid plan in place to turn the vision into a reality. When it comes to leadership reputations, there are only two: good reputations and bad reputations. Anything in the middle is not a reputation. To clarify their approach, leaders need to ask themselves, "Do I want to be liked or do I want to be respected?" To ensure you are cultivating respect, ask yourself

- "What is my leadership legacy?"
- "What do I hope the people who work for me will say about me as a leader?"
- "What actions do I need to take on a daily basis to earn high levels of respect from my boss, direct reports, peers, and customers?"

People are motivated to follow people they respect, and your personal leadership vision needs to focus on cultivating respect rather than being well-liked.

Deliver Results

Our mail arrives pretty much every day, with very few

exceptions, regardless of weather conditions. Our postal carriers deliver in rain, sleet, ice, snow, wind, or intense heat. They get the job done and deliver results. Respected leaders figure out how to overcome the obstacles, build relationships to get the job done, and deliver results.

Communicate Honestly, Directly, and in a Timely Manner

Respected leaders are consistent in their communication. They are honest, direct, and timely, even when the recipient may not be happy with the information communicated. Leaders are respected for delivering the same message with the same key points to everyone, regardless of whether the people happen to like the message or the leader.

> *Leaders are respected for delivering the same message with the same key points to everyone, regardless of whether the people happen to like the message or the leader.*

Treat Everyone with Respect

It is easy to be respectful when others treat you with respect. It is much more difficult to be respectful when others treat you in a manner you interpret as questioning your authority, failing to communicate important information that prevents you from doing your job, or communicating in a condescending and demeaning manner. These behaviors fall under the umbrella of disrespectful behavior. When leaders are faced with these situations, it is critical they remain calm and respond respectfully and professionally. Most often, others know when a team member is being disrespectful. When you take the high road and avoid responding inappropriately, you earn respect.

Create an Organizational Structure Based on the Organization's Needs, Not Employees' Personalities

To be respected as a leader, you need to make good decisions. One of a leader's most important decisions is to create an organizational structure that best serves the organization and successfully accomplishes the mission and vision. Determining an organizational structure might sound easy, but leaders are often faced with some pushback from unhappy employees. Leaders need to make tough decisions that are right for the team and the organization, not an individual employee's happiness.

Lean into Conflict

Great leaders understand conflict can actually be positive and lead people and teams to better outcomes. Leaders who lean into conflict view a difference of opinion as healthy and helpful to ensure they consider all angles and possibilities when resolving problems.

Some drawn-out, acrimonious conflicts, however, can become destructive. Anytime there is a conflict between two people that cannot be resolved, one or both team members have, most likely, contributed significantly to the escalation of the conflict. A respected leader requires the two team members to sit down and resolve the conflict, or one or both team members may be asked to leave the organization. One or both of the team members will not be happy about the face-to-face meeting with the other team member and will hope the leader will forget about this meeting. A respected leader is resolute in resolving destructive conflicts.

Be Friendly, Be Caring … But Don't Be Friends with Your Direct Reports

This is a point many of our clients like to debate. They

strongly believe you can be friends with your direct reports, and other employees should accept the fact. When you are close friends with your reports, it makes it much more difficult to make business decisions that are not swayed by emotions. It is also difficult to claim you are unbiased and fair to all employees if you regularly spend time away from work with your employee friends. It blurs the lines and is unfair to the employee. This certainly does not mean you should not be friendly and caring towards each and every one of your direct reports. Hopefully, they will be friendly and caring in return. Strong leaders understand the difference between being friendly and being friends, and they respect the boundary between the two.

Recognize That Equal and Fair Are Two Different Issues

Some of your direct reports may take more of your time to coach and mentor than others. That means your time is not divided up equally among your team members, but that does not make you an unfair leader. Fair leaders are equally committed to each team member's success and puts in the time and effort required, even if that varies from team member to team member.

Be Consistent and Fair

Respected leaders do not show favoritism. If you are going to go to lunch with one employee, either invite the other employees along or make time in the future to take every team member to lunch. Leaders who appear to favor certain employees and treat team members inconsistently lose respect and foster resentment within their teams.

Hold All Team Members Accountable for Their Responsibilities

When you have different standards for different team

members, it is harder for team members to respect you as a just leader. This becomes especially apparent when some team members are given benefits and rewards that are not also offered to other team members achieving similar results.

Provide Honest Credit and Recognition

It is easy to withhold positive feedback when some team members are not doing what you need them to do or are difficult to deal with. A respected leader provides positive feedback and finds a reason to celebrate when someone does great work, makes a good suggestion, or makes a positive contribution to the team's success — even if this employee can be difficult. Try framing positive feedback to your most difficult employee as "I am so grateful you are on my team. I know when we implement changes, you provide alternatives and options. I need you to know that helps me to be an even stronger leader and develops us as a team."

7 Tips for Earning Respect

1. It is more important to be respected than to be liked.
2. Some team members are not good fits for their roles. Help them find other places to work.
3. Design an organizational structure based on functions and not personalities.
4. Lean into conflict. Conflict can be positive in leading teams to even better outcomes.
5. Hold people accountable.
6. Create an environment where employees find it easy to be engaged.
7. Make decisions in the best interest of the team or organization.

Their Confidence Becomes Arrogance

Confidence is believing in yourself.
Arrogance is telling others you're better than they are.
Confidence inspires. Arrogance destroys.

—Simon Sinek

During a recent executive team meeting, we facilitated a discussion about the large number of information technology-related failures the company was experiencing. At one point in the meeting, the CEO asked the CIO, "By what date can we expect these problems to be resolved?" The CIO abruptly stated, "I can't give you a date." The CEO pressed the CIO for more information. "You have to give us some hope for a resolution. Give us a ballpark timeframe. Are we talking ninety days, six months, a year, or even two years?" The CIO angrily responded, in front of the rest of the executive team, "I am the smartest person in this room when it comes to technology, and I'm telling you I don't know when the problems will be fixed. If I don't know, then nobody knows." Silence filled the room.

Every person in that room was thinking, "If I were the CEO, I would fire you right now and find someone who *can* tell me when and how these problems will be resolved."

There's a fine line between confidence and arrogance. When leaders are confident, they have a deep belief in their ability to make a difference in the world. Confidence is an important competency in leadership, and it is critical to their success. Confidence is motivating and inspirational to others. It gives them the ability to take the risks needed to stay innovative and push the team or organization further ahead.

Arrogance happens when confidence morphs into cockiness: "I am so fantastic you cannot live without me!" then into recklessness, "I can do whatever I want!" then into arrogance, "I can do what I want because I am untouchable!"

> *Arrogance crosses the line of confidence.*

Arrogance crosses the line of confidence. Arrogant people believe they no longer have a need to learn, grow, or change. They wholeheartedly believe they are right and others are wrong.

Arrogance destroys the valuable, and absolutely essential, relationships a leader has with other team members. Even more devastating is the feeling arrogant behavior creates in others. People have no desire or motivation to follow an arrogant leader. Sometimes the arrogance is so repugnant that people cheer when arrogant people fail, even if it means they suffer, too.

Path to Failure

Arrogant leaders embody several traits and behaviors that are detrimental to their leadership success.

Believing They Are Smarter

Arrogant individuals truly believe they are the smartest person in the organization.

Bernie Madoff, who orchestrated the largest financial fraud in history with his Ponzi scheme, defrauded his clients for over forty years. The Securities Investment Protection Corporation estimates the actual loss to investors was $18 billion. Why did he do it? He didn't think he would be caught. He was so supremely arrogant he believed he was smarter than everyone in the SEC.

Some arrogant leaders believe they are smarter because of their formal education, their degrees, or their ability. The belief that one is smarter than others is especially prevalent in "smart" organizations such as universities, technology firms, hospitals, school districts, and law firms.

What we learned from leaders in these highly educated industries is rather fascinating. If other people agree with arrogant leaders, they are considered by those leaders to be smart and well-educated. If people question the leader's decisions or recommendations, they are often labeled as unintelligent. For an arrogant leader, disagreement equals ignorance. Many arrogant leaders have gone so far as to call others in the organization stupid when they dare to challenge or question the leader.

When this happens, subordinates and peers learn not to challenge the leader, even when he or she is clearly wrong. Not only do arrogant leaders belittle those who disagree with them, but they often do so in the most condescending and patronizing way possible.

It is difficult to work for an arrogant person, but it is also difficult having one work for you. When people believe they are smarter than their bosses, they frequently fail to follow directions, refuse guidance, and ignore feedback.

Bragging

What is the fastest way for leaders to quickly alienate their teams when they are new on the job? Tell your team how great your last organization or job was and all the wonderful things you accomplished there. If you want to put icing on the cake, tell your team that, if they do what you tell them to, they could be as great as your last team was. When you tell people about your fantastic past, it leaves your team members with three burning questions:

- If your last team was so good, why did you leave?
- If your last organization was so good, why don't you go back?
- When are you leaving?

Believing It's All About Them

Arrogant people feel best when they talk about themselves. Let's face it, most of us do, but, arrogant people excel at taking normal human interaction into the truly narcissistic realm. They love to talk about their dreams, goals, and accomplishments. They are not comfortable listening, asking questions, or holding a conversation about other topics. Arrogant people are good at giving advice (whether solicited or not), but not at accepting advice from others. In fact, if you do happen to broach a topic the arrogant person does not agree with or see value in, they are quite comfortable cutting you off mid-sentence so they can control the conversation once again.

Lacking Listening Skills

Arrogant people take pride in multi-tasking. Instead of taking the time to stop what they are doing, make eye contact, and truly listen to the person talking to them, arrogant leaders continue responding to their emails, making notes, eating lunch, or completing other tasks. They love looking at other things instead of making eye contact while you are speaking to them. They are very busy thinking about other things and clearly demonstrate they have far more important issues to attend to than you.

> *Arrogant leaders clearly communicate they are too busy for you.*

Ignoring Accountability

Arrogant leaders are quick to provide excuses when they do not do what they said they were going to do or do not deliver the desired results. Almost always, the excuses point to things they cannot control. Excuses, such as the economy is bad, they are overburdened, or another team member stopped them from successfully completing their projects on time, are common among managers who lack accountability.

Being Unwilling to Admit They Are Wrong

Arrogant managers have a very difficult time saying "I was wrong" or "I did not handle that well." They often feel a need to explain why others are wrong and they are right. The whole team and organization is messed up, according to these arrogant managers, and that is why they need to take the actions they do.

Being Unable to Apologize

Arrogant managers have a hard time admitting they are wrong, and an even harder time saying "I'm sorry. I promise I won't do it again." We have even witnessed leaders who yelled and swore at other team members. When someone told one of these leaders he needed to apologize for his poor behavior and lack of professionalism, he responded, "I'm not apologizing to anyone. He (the recipient of the yelling) was wrong for provoking me, and you (the person asking him to apologize) are wrong for not standing up to him when you knew he was wrong." Everyone else is always wrong.

Rejecting Feedback

If you have ever tried to give an arrogant person constructive criticism or guidance, you know the feedback is not appreciated. Negative feedback makes arrogant people upset and angry. "How dare my boss tell me I am wrong!" They usually respond in a way that sends a strong message they do not ever want feedback again. The reactions vary from anger to completely ceasing any and all communication with you. Either way, the impact is the same; you think twice before you give them feedback.

Believing Their Needs Are More Important

Arrogant people feel they should be prioritized. They cut in front of others when there is a line. They disrupt a conversation between others because they feel their need at that moment is more important. They answer their phone when they are in the middle of a conversation with someone else or in the check-out line at the grocery store. And our favorite: the people who push past others to get off the plane first.

Engaging in One-Upmanship

Arrogant leaders love to tell others about all the wonderful things they have accomplished and acquired. No matter what others have seen or done, arrogant people always have a story about a time they did it bigger and better. They caught a bigger fish. They have a newer, faster car. They love to tell you about their latest exotic vacation, especially after you tell them you spent your vacation sick in the hospital. "Oh, sorry you couldn't go anywhere. Did you know we spent ten days in Costa Rica?"

Withholding Praise and Recognition

Arrogant leaders are quick to tell you how wonderful they are and all the great things they have accomplished, but they tend to withhold praise and recognition when others do great work or are successful. It is hard for them to believe others are worthy of attention and recognition.

Undermining Their Boss

You might question why this point would show up in arrogance. Here's why: Arrogant people truly believe they are smarter and make better decisions than their bosses. They never stop to think, "Someone higher up must believe my boss has significant value and creates important outcomes for the team or organization." For example, your boss's boss really trusts your boss and the decisions he makes. Or, maybe your boss's boss thinks your boss is doing a great job. Arrogant people fail to understand they are just as disposable as everyone else. When you undermine your boss, you will more often than not find yourself unemployed.

Not Valuing Continuous Learning

When arrogant people believe they are the smartest person in the room, their unwillingness to learn, grow, and change gives them a false sense of their abilities in other areas of life. They may be the smartest person in an area of expertise, but when it comes to emotional intelligence and building strong relationships with others, they may fail miserably. Arrogant people truly believe they know it all. They do not.

Communicating Disrespectfully

Arrogant leaders might as well wear a sign proclaiming "I am arrogant!" An arrogant leader is easy to identify by his communication style, both verbal and nonverbal. When things don't go their way in a conversation, they raise their voices, swear for impact, or put people down in front of others. In one meeting we facilitated, the leader dramatically rolled her eyes when a team member made a recommendation to solve a problem. In another situation, we saw a leader walk away from their direct report while the direct report was still talking to him. To make matters worse, the leader held up his hand in exasperation to emphasize "I have heard enough from you." The employee shut down, stopped contributing, and eventually left for another job.

Prescription for Confident Success

Of the seven reasons why leaders fail, arrogance is one of the most difficult to work with and overcome. As we mentioned in an earlier chapter, there are only two types of reputations: good reputations and bad reputations. Anything in the middle is leadership gray matter, not a reputation. The good news is that, with focused effort and hard work, you can change your reputation from one of arrogance to one of servant leadership and humility. Here's how:

Admit Mistakes

When you have a genuine desire to learn, it is much easier to admit you have made a mistake or did not handle something as well as it could have been handled. We witnessed a great example of this in a meeting we facilitated. The leader stated, "When I walked into this meeting today, I came in to tell everyone I was adamantly opposed to hiring Jane. After listening to everyone's reasoning, I think I'm wrong and I've changed my mind. Find out when she can start, and let me know what I can do to help expedite the hiring and budgeting process." Admitting mistakes and changing course is better than continuing down the wrong path.

Apologize

Part of admitting you are wrong includes making amends and apologizing. Sincerely showing remorse for past behaviors and attitudes can go a long way toward creating more harmonious relationships.

We are talking about genuine apologies here, not the "I'm sorry you feel that way" or "I'm sorry you misinterpreted what I said" pseudo-apologies. Those are not apologies; they are words intended to shift the blame back onto the other person, and score you zero points.

Help Others Succeed

When people see your willingness to take the time to help others, the same people you have helped feel a stronger commitment to helping you accomplish the vision and goals you have for the team. It is important to note that being a humble leader does not mean you are an enabling pushover leader who is unable to achieve your own goals. It means you are a strong leader, committed to helping people achieve their fullest potential by mentoring, encouraging, and pushing them toward success. Great leaders consider other people before they consider themselves.

Honor Their Current Team

One of the worst things a leader can do is gloat about their past accomplishments or how great their former team or organization was. If you transfer from the Indianapolis Colts to the Denver Broncos, but you constantly talk about how great the Colts were, you discourage your new team. Keep in mind that your current organization and team invited you to the dance by hiring you. Instead of putting down the way things have been done in the past, honor their past by acknowledging their accomplishments. Then, share with them your vision and help the team build a sturdy bridge to the future.

Be Grateful

Would the people you live and work with describe you as a grateful person? George Burns, who lived to be 100 years old, once said, "The first thing I do each morning is check the obituary section of the paper. If my name is not in it, I know it's going to be a great day." We both practice gratitude exercises. We note what we are grateful for, and we find this daily practice boosts attitude, decreases stress, and helps us mentally prepare for the day.

Are you grateful to be alive? Are you grateful for the people in your family and in your life? Are you grateful for the ability to do the job you do and lead the people on your team?

When you are a grateful leader, it is much easier to see the good in others and provide ample praise and recognition where it is due. Gratitude builds relationships. Think about how you have been blessed, as well as whom and what you are grateful for in your life. Humble leaders are good at letting others know they are appreciated and valued for the contributions they make every day.

Divert Attention

When someone praises a humble leader, that leader is quick to say something along the lines of, "I'm grateful for the positive feedback and I am very proud to be the leader of this team. But, I need everyone to know the great work you are thanking me for is the result of our great team. Specifically, I need to recognize Morgan and John, who have led this project from the beginning. I will pass along your feedback to each of them, and I hope that, if you do speak or meet with them, you can provide them with the same feedback you just gave me. I am blessed to lead such a great team."

We were recently part of a 1,000-person recognition ceremony for a client, and she said, "I get the praise but I'm really just a figurehead. There is no way we could succeed without each member of the team." And she named each of her team members by name. The CEO said to the crowd, "Now that's a real leader!"

Be Accountable

When the team makes a mistake, a strong leader accepts accountability for the mistake and takes responsibility for ensuring the problem never happens again. An arrogant leader would deny any wrongdoing and say, "I was not responsible for this mistake." In fact, he or she would probably tell you exactly who was responsible for the mistake. Humble leaders know that if it happened on your team, you are ultimately responsible. They also know they do not have to say they personally made the mistake. What they do need to do is be accountable for the mistake and ensure the problem or concern is properly resolved.

> *Wins belong to the team. Mistakes belong to you.*

Be Focused and Forgiving

When someone makes a mistake, humble leaders focus on resolving the problem. They will do whatever they can to help improve the situation, and all their energy is future focused. They are trying to answer two important questions:

1. Where do we need to be?

2. What actions can we take to improve the situation and get to where we want to be most expeditiously?

Just as quickly as they are able to focus their positive energy on the future, they are able to forgive. Being a forgiving leader in critical situations is one of the best ways to build strong relationships in which people are highly motivated to follow you.

Demonstrate Respect

Humble leaders show respect to everyone.

A candidate for a VP job reached the final question of the interview. He was the clear front runner for the job. He had been at the company for seven years, and he was well-liked. But, this question stumped him: "What is the name of the security guard you pass every morning?" He didn't know. He lost the promotion.

Many leaders find it easy to reciprocate respectful behavior. The true test for humble leaders presents itself when others treat them in a disrespectful manner. How would you respond if a direct report rolled their eyes in front of other team members when you proposed a new change for your team? That is the real test of humility. Humble leaders have the ability to demonstrate respect, even in the most challenging of situations.

Ask for Feedback

Humble leaders are comfortable asking for feedback and acting on it when appropriate. Because humble leaders are confident, they do not feel the need to collect only glowing feedback to validate their worthiness. Rather, they collect honest feedback to better understand themselves, determine new actions, and become stronger leaders in the process. Great leaders recognize not everyone will like or agree with their decisions and they are comfortable with disagreement. These leaders know that, through feedback, they may learn of better ways to communicate, develop a product, or implement a decision.

Learn Continuously

If arrogant leaders are defined by the belief they no longer need to learn anything new, then humble leaders are defined as lifelong learners. Great leaders are continuously trying to figure out how they can improve in all areas of their lives.

Humble leaders believe they can be a better partner to their significant other; be a better parent to their children; gain more expertise in their chosen field; and be a better leader, who is able to lead teams that enjoy extraordinary success. In his book, *Drucker on Asia*, Peter Drucker wrote that, every three years, he picked a new subject to learn about. For more than sixty years, he studied one subject at a time. That not only gave him a substantial fund of knowledge, it also forced him to be open to new disciplines, new approaches, and new methods — for every one of the subjects he studied makes different assumptions and employs a different methodology.

Recognize Success

Humble leaders habitually recognize great contributions that make a difference. At home, at work, and in their daily routines, great leaders find it easy to say "thank you" and recognize someone for how they make a difference in this world.

7 Tips for Projecting Confidence, Not Arrogance

1. Admit and accept that you make mistakes, and apologize for them.
2. Demonstrate accountability and take responsibility for the actions of your team.
3. Communicate and act in a respectful manner at all times.
4. Be open-minded and willing to learn something new.
5. Show gratitude and give praise and recognition where it is due.
6. Practice forgiveness.
7. Ask for honest feedback, and act on it.

Conclusion

Are You a Coachable—
and a Coach-Able—Leader?

*A good head and a good heart are a
formidable combination.*

—Nelson Mandela

We recently had a conversation with an executive coach who was new to the business and we asked her a direct question, "What is your rate of success with coaching managers?" This new consultant immediately shot back, "100 percent successful! Every person I coach benefits and succeeds from my expertise." We should have been more specific with how we defined coaching success. This new consultant believed if any of her clients witnessed the slightest improvement, then that improvement qualified as success. She had no real metrics, such as 360-feedback, for measuring success.

Our standards are higher. Sometimes the leaders we coach put what they learn in their coaching sessions into action and go on to build stronger teams and produce better results. These leaders are promoted to higher levels within the organization and take on more responsibility. Others times, the leaders do not take action on the coaching they receive. Eventually, their boss and others in the organization realize they are in the wrong job, the wrong industry, or they have the wrong employees; their supervisor decides it is time for the leader who is being coached to move on.

These less successful leaders suffer from what we call the Popeye Syndrome. Popeye was famous for the phase "I am what I am." These Popeyes tend to blame their challenges and problems on someone or something else. They don't see how their actions and behaviors contribute to the challenges. Leaders with this mindset are difficult to coach because, at heart, they do not want to change. They are not very coachable because they resist taking responsibility to take the necessary actions to solve their problems.

Interestingly enough, these same managers who are not open to coaching are also those who resist helping and mentoring others. As reflected in the title of this chapter, leaders who are not coachable are also incapable of coaching others. It's often said that the best teachers are, first and foremost, great learners.

At the heart of great leadership is the commitment of these leaders to their own continuous improvement, as well as to the improvement of those around them. Leadership coaching is about accepting feedback and utilizing that feedback to improve leadership abilities, which translates into better vision, communication, teamwork, relationships, productivity, and ultimately, better profits for the organization.

Whether or not you are assigned a coach, or you are coaching others, make sure that first, you're a leader who is genuinely committed to learn and grow in your role, and second, you're a leader who ensures your direct reports are equally committed to learn and grow in their roles. This is a big key to your next promotion.

You Might Be an Uncoachable Leader If ...

Where do you stand? Perhaps you believe sincerely that all is well: you embrace learning from others and those around you are eager to learn from you. In truth, however, you may be less coachable — and less coach-able — than you believe. Here are the five warning signs of an uncoachable leader:

1. **They think they are smarter than others.** There is nothing wrong with believing you are smart and having confidence in your abilities. But, when you truly believe you're smarter than your boss, or your boss's boss, you quickly lose the motivation to learn, grow, and change from the feedback you receive. Your actions usually come across as disrespectful. When others perceive you as disrespectful, you are not doing your career or your teams any favors.

2. **They don't listen.** Uncoachable managers tend to not listen very well. Strong leaders ask questions and seek to understand others' points of view and expand their own. Uncoachable managers, on the other hand, have a pressing need to tell you exactly why their actions are right, and are not willing to admit or consider this might not be the case.

3. **Their egos are bigger than their brains.** Uncoachable managers usually know what their boss wants them to do and what actions, if taken, will help them be successful. Even though they know what they need to do, they are sabotaged by their own egos. They might make ego-based decisions to not communicate important information to their boss, or to not follow through on their boss' requests or directions.

4. **They don't care.** These managers don't care what others think of their behaviors. We recently informed a manager that six people on his team had described

him as a bully. Instead of saying "Wow, being a bully has never been my goal; let's figure out what I can do differently," this manager stated, "If I need to be a bully to get stuff done, so be it." This manager, though incredibly smart in the IQ sense, severely lacked EQ, or Emotional Intelligence. EQ, rather than IQ, will always be the deciding factor in your next promotion. Understanding and caring about people and what they think is a big piece of any leader's future success.

5. **They have a pressing need to be right.** My dad gave me a great piece of advice about marriage. He told me, "If you want your marriage to last, you need to make a really important decision. Do you want to be right, or do you want to be happy?" In your personal relationship, hopefully, you make the decision that being happy together is more important than being right. You don't quibble over small things.

The same principle is equally applicable in business. Some of these uncoachable managers would be much better off being employed and happy, rather than being right and unemployed. In so many instances in life, little issues and being strident about inconsequential matters are not as important as nurturing strong relationships that allow you to move your goals forward.

The Ten Skills of Coachable Leaders

If you're still reading this book, chances are you're not an uncoachable manager. But, it is helpful to review the ten critical skills successful leaders put into action to continuously learn, improve, and be the person that people choose to follow.

All professional athletes have coaches. Every Little League team has coaches. Coaches are a resource for those who want to improve. We marvel at the fact that some businesspeople believe they don't need coaching. We understand some people who have had bad coaches are reluctant to either coach or be coached. However, we believe the highest performing executives have boards of advisors, confidants, and coaches who help them strive to improve their leadership skills.

True professionals embrace opportunities to further their careers and become better leaders.

1. **Have a clear and compelling vision.** Coachable managers have a positive vision of the improvements they can make as a leader. They deeply believe they can improve the condition of their team or organization. Coachable leaders believe they will become stronger leaders by taking advantage of any opportunity to learn and better themselves as leaders. They have a compelling positive vision that motivates others on the team to also believe in the vision, stay focused on the big picture, and take the necessary actions to turn that vision into a reality.

2. **Genuinely Care.** Coachable leaders genuinely care about the wellbeing and success of others. Great leaders demonstrate they care by taking the necessary time to communicate important information as well as listen to the ideas and concerns of their team. More importantly, coachable leaders act on the information they gain from team members.

3. **Build Trust.** The biggest difference between a manager and a leader is that a leader may or may not have a formal title and a place on the organizational chart but always has a relationship where people willingly follow them. People do not follow people they do not respect or trust.

When it comes to trust, it is a catch 22: you either trust people or you don't. Either way, you are usually right. If you trust people, you usually delegate freely, clarify expectations and outcomes, and then you stand back and let people do their jobs. If you do not trust people, you tend to withhold information and not delegate important tasks. And when you do delegate, you micro-manage employees because you don't trust that, without your oversight, they will do things the way you want them done. The allocation of trust is like a self-fulfilling prophecy: what you believe will happen, will happen. If you don't trust your people, they will meet your low expectations and not be trustworthy. If you trust your people, they will reward your trust by being trustworthy. It's your decision.

Coachable leaders first trust themselves. Knowing they can be successful and resilient leaders when faced with setbacks, coachable leaders also have trust in their team members and know that, with the right coaching and leadership, they have what it takes to get the job done.

4. **Ask for feedback.** Great managers ask, "What can I do as a leader to better support you in getting your job done?" Coachable leaders are also good at sharing their challenges with their coach and asking for advice on how to handle the challenges. Although coachable leaders do not accept or act on all feedback they receive, they are excellent at looking for patterns and themes in the feedback they receive, and then taking the appropriate actions that will take their leadership skills to a higher level.

5. **Be humble.** Whether at home or at work, life is a whole lot easier when you can say, "I screwed

up. If I had to do that again, I wouldn't take the same actions. I'm sorry for my part in this." When managers have the ability to admit their mistakes, they take the targets off their backs. When managers feel compelled to justify why they did something that was clearly wrong, others feel a higher level of motivation to prove them wrong. Coachable leaders know they do not have all the answers. They will make mistakes, but they take pride in giving others credit for the team's success.

6. **Be respected.** Coachable managers know that being a great leader is difficult. Leadership is all about improving the condition of the team or organization and improvement means change. We all know many people are not excited about change. The great line, "I like change but you go first," is so true. What gets leaders into trouble faster than anything is when they have a higher need to be liked than to be respected. When you make a change, you know not everyone will like either you or your proposed change. Knowing this and being willing to ride the J-Curve is important knowledge in the business of leadership. As the changes take hold and the condition of your team or organization begins to improve, the people will come around: most people respect leaders who produce positive results.

7. **Be fair.** Coachable leaders are fair in everything they do. They are consistent in how they make decisions and how they set standards. They are consistent in their moods. They are equitable and fair in how they treat people. They are comfortable giving praise, recognition, and credit when it is due. Coachable leaders are quick to forgive themselves and others when things do not go as planned.

8. **Build a united team.** Coachable leaders recognize that, to be successful, you need a united team. Although most leaders are successful in building their own teams, building teamwork cross-departmentally is a bigger challenge. Great leaders know that, whether you work cross-departmentally or across divisions, they have the responsibility to build one team and hold all team members accountable to work in alignment with the mission and vision of the organization.

9. **Be proactive.** Strong leaders are proactive rather than reactive. For instance, coachable managers will call their coach when things do not go as well as planned. Uncoachable leaders, however, will avoid contacting their coach, and the first time the coach hears of a problem is when the boss of the individual being coached makes contact with the coach and informs him that things have not gone well. Coachable managers contact the coach first and say, "This did not work out very well. Let's talk and figure out the best strategy moving forward."

10. **Be comfortable with being uncomfortable.** Most changes we make in life are uncomfortable. Driving to an unknown location is uncomfortable. Even moving your watch from your left arm and placing it on your right arm for the rest of the day is uncomfortable. We recently asked a manager described as impersonal and cold to greet each of her team members with a simple "Good morning" or "How is your day going?" This manager told us, "This is the most difficult and awkward thing I have ever done." To be a coachable leader, you need to be willing to change your behaviors and that, most likely, will be uncomfortable.

Strong leaders know their career development trajectory depends on their willingness to adapt, learn, and grow. Or, as Clint Eastwood said in the movie *Heartbreak Ridge*, leaders need to "adapt, overcome, and improvise." We need to adjust, solve problems, and devise creative solutions that utilize our people's best talents. Feedback comes in many forms, not just through executive coaching. Whether or not you're working with an executive coach, make sure you're receptive to learning and growing in your leadership role. Be both a leader who accepts coaching and one who coaches and mentors others. Create a culture of continuous improvement, unending development, and a work environment that fosters trust and encourages ideas.

Great leadership is not easy. Will you be successful in becoming a stronger and more effective leader? If you have the positive vision, the willingness to take feedback, the strong desire to learn, and the determination to put what you learn into action and do the right thing, you will succeed. As the kids say to each other when they are trying to accomplish something really difficult ... YOU'VE GOT THIS!

We wish you great success!

Peter and Mary

7 Ways to Engage

Leaders and organizations that want to achieve greatness plan to improve themselves and their people. We have a variety of tools to help individuals, teams, and organizations succeed.

1. Engage your employees with an employee opinion survey.

We have surveyed over 150 organizations and over 150,000 employees and managers around the world. We have the right assessments to make it simple and easy for organizations to measure employee engagement. We deliver a customized report broken down by department to give leaders an overall picture of the organization as well as to show the organization where it is most effective and where there are opportunities for improvement.

We specialize in helping organizations build cultures where employees love to come to work!

2. Engage your managers with our leadership development programs:

- Leadership Lessons for Supervisors and Managers
- Leadership Challenges in Today's Workforce
- How to Build, Lead, and Keep High-Performing Teams
- Relationship Strategies—Dealing With Different Types of People
- Communicating Effectively for Maximum Results
- 15 Ways to Grow Your Business in Every Economy
- Effectively Leading Organizational Change
- Negotiation Skills—Creating Win-Win Outcomes
- Coaching and Counseling for Improved Performance
- Performance Management
- Conflict Resolution
- Building Effective Teams: Team-building Strategies from the Military

3. Engage your employees with our training programs, addressing:

- Survive and Thrive During Times of Change
- Communication Skills
- Time Management: Maximize Personal and Professional Productivity
- Presentation Skills
- Dealing With Difficult People/Customers
- Conflict Resolution
- Team Building
- Deliver Extraordinary Customer Service

4. Engage your leaders with a 360-degree leadership development assessment evaluation.

Our Leadership Development Assessment is an organizational tool to help managers and leaders become more effective by increasing their self-awareness and self-understanding. The LDA works on the principle of multilevel feedback and provides a comparative profile of the managers' leadership skills as observed by others. This feedback provides a personal portrait of each manager's strengths and areas for improvement. Our consultants create customized recommendations and an Action Plan for these managers to become stronger, more effective leaders.

We have provided a sample of the Leadership Development Assessment designed specifically for the readers of this book.

5. Engage your leaders with our executive coaching programs.

We provide customized plans to help leaders reach their full potential. Leaders in our coaching programs say they discover their true purpose and passion, and they develop the skills necessary to build lasting relationships and strong organizations. Our coaching clients claim that working with us saves them time and resources, improves morale, and allows them to confidently lead their teams to new levels of success.

6. Engage your executive leaders and senior management:
- Executive Leadership Strategies
- Strategic Leadership Retreats
- Strategic Planning Facilitation
- Conflict Resolution
- Team Building
- Executive Team Assessments

7. Engage your team with one of our keynote speeches:

- Effectively Lead Organizational Change
- Survive and Thrive: Change Management
- How to Build, Lead, and Keep High-Performing Teams
- Engaged—Building an Organization Where Employees Love to Come to Work
- Win-Win Negotiations
- Lifetime Leadership—Leaving a Legacy

For more information about any of these engagement options, please contact us. We'd love to hear from you!

Peter B. Stark
www.PeterStark.com
Peter@PeterStark.com
858-451-3601

To connect with Peter online:
Tweet him @PeterBStark
Like him at facebook.com/PeterBarronStarkCompanies
Connect with him at LinkedIn.com/in/PeterBStark
Follow his blog at www.PeterStark.com/blog

Mary C. Kelly
www.ProductiveLeaders.com
Mary@ProductiveLeaders.com
719-357-7360

To connect with Mary online:
Tweet her @MaryKellySpeaks
Like her at facebook.com/in/DrMaryKelly
Connect with her on LinkedIn.com/in/DrMaryKelly
Follow her blog at www.ProductiveLeaders.com/blog

Appendix

Take Your Free Leadership Development Self-Assessment Online

With the purchase of this book, you also receive a free mini Leadership Development Self-Assessment (LDSA) to evaluate your current level of leadership skills. This tool was designed based on the skills outlined in the book and is intended to help managers at all levels become more effective by increasing their self-awareness and self-understanding.

Not only will you gain knowledge on how you see yourself, but you will also be provided with a benchmark comparison. Upon completion, you will be able to compare your results to our Overall Benchmark in addition to our Best of the Best Benchmark data of over 475 leaders. These benchmarks provide a metric for you to identify your areas of leadership effectiveness, as well as your opportunities for improvement.

When you have the assessment in hand, you will have powerful information on what you need to do as a leader to take your leadership to the next level. You will also have the "how to" in the form of the tools presented in the book.

So, let's get started.

The mini LDSA contains 36 questions and should only take a few minutes to complete.

1. To access the leadership assessment, visit:
   http://bit.ly/1O3X7DO

2. After you have completed the assessment, your results will be emailed to you in a PDF format.

When you receive your results, you will have a great picture of your strengths and your opportunities for improvement. Be sure to celebrate the areas where you score high in addition to identifying the areas you would like to work on. Each area will be linked to a section of the book where you can learn more to expand your knowledge and grow your leadership skills. Knowing your strengths and opportunities for improvement and committing to improve your lowest areas will allow you to become more confident in your abilities, build stronger workplace relationships, and succeed as a leader.